# Bella Caledonia

D0819323

# Scottish Cultural Review of Language and Literature

## Volume 11

Series Editors
Rhona Brown
*University of Glasgow*

John Corbett
*University of Glasgow*

Sarah Dunnigan
*University of Edinburgh*

James McGonigal
*University of Glasgow*

Production Editor
Ronnie Young
*University of Glasgow*

SCROLL

The Scottish Cultural Review of Language and Literature publishes new work in Scottish Studies, with a focus on analysis and reinterpretation of the literature and languages of Scotland, and the cultural contexts that have shaped them.

Further information on our editorial and production procedures can be found at www.rodopi.nl

# Bella Caledonia
## Woman, Nation, Text

Kirsten Stirling

Amsterdam - New York, NY 2008

Cover image:
'The Drunk Man's Wife' by Virginia Colley. With kind permission of
Dr. Elspeth King of the Stirling Smith Art Gallery and Museum.

Cover design: Gavin Miller and Pier Post

The paper on which this book is printed meets the requirements of "ISO
9706: 1994, Information and documentation - Paper for documents -
Requirements for permanence".

ISBN: 978-90-420-2510-3
©Editions Rodopi B.V., Amsterdam - New York, NY 2008
Printed in The Netherlands

*For Moira Burgess*

# Contents

Acknowledgements                                                      9

Introduction:      *Engendering the Nation*                          11

Chapter One:       *Woman as Nation*                                 15

Chapter Two:       *The Female Figure in the Scottish Renaissance*   35

Chapter Three:     *The Female Nation as Victim*                     65

Chapter Four:      *The Monstrous Muse*                              87

Chapter Five:      *Women Writing Nation*                           109

Bibliography                                                        127

Index                                                               135

# Acknowledgements

This book started off as a thesis written in the Department of Scottish Literature at the University of Glasgow. I would like to thank all the colleagues and friends there who encouraged and supported me, including Christopher Whyte and Douglas Gifford. In the journey from thesis to book a lot has changed; for that stage of the process I would like to thank friends and colleagues from the University of Lausanne, especially Lucy Perry, Didier Maillat and Neil Forsyth. Thanks also to Sarah Dunnigan and the editorial team at SCROLL. Thank you also to Peter Stirling, particularly for his inspired suggestions for epigraphs, even if they didn't get used in the end. Special thanks to Ian MacKenzie, without whose close reading and strong-arm encouragement neither thesis nor book might ever have seen the light of day. Finally, thanks to my mum, Moira Burgess, for giving me every possible kind of support all through my education and beyond; I would like to dedicate this book to her.

# Introduction

## Engendering the Nation

Whenever gender and nation collide, whether this involves the representation of the nation as gendered, or the concomitant role of women as citizens, complications appear. One of the most obvious and visible ways of gendering the nation is the familiar practice of representing the nation itself in the form of a woman, a symbol which is ingrained in European tradition and, judging by its widespread use, has a great deal of attraction. This use of the female figure elevates and semi-deifies women on the symbolic level but can contribute to disenfranchising them from the position of citizen on a practical level. The symbolic elevation appears to value women's role in the nation but it masks the political powerlessness of actual women.

These problems surrounding the personification of the nation are present in Scotland, but in a peculiar form, because the Scottish version of the woman-as-nation figure does not really emerge until the twentieth century, and even then in a much more muted form than some of her better-known counterparts, such as Britannia, Marianne (in France) or Helvetia (in Switzerland). Histories of these more established female figureheads trace their institutional significance and survey different ways in which the female figure may represent the nation, whether enshrined in official iconography of the nation or used in popular cartoons and caricatures (Warner 1996: 3–60; Dresser 1989; Agulhon 1979, 1989; Kreis 1991; Cusack and Bhreathnach-Lynch 2003).

In Scotland, the situation is different for a number of reasons. Firstly, since the very status of Scotland as a nation is problematic, particularly before the devolved parliament of 1999, any Scottish figurehead would not represent an independent political state but a less rigidly defined entity, autonomous in some respects but subordinate to the British government. For this reason, there is no history of the institutional use of a female Scotland – on civic architecture, on banknotes, or on any other signifiers of national identity – and no strong tradition of representing Scotland visually as a woman. When woman-as-nation figures can be identified for the first time in Scotland, in the early twentieth century, they appear in literature rather than the visual arts, adding a new layer of interpretative problems. Much of the vocabulary and methodology established to describe figures such as Marianne and Britannia relate to their visual incarnations. In *Monuments and Maidens* (1996), Marina Warner approaches "the allegory of the female form" through visual examples: the statue of Liberty, busts of Marianne and caricatures of Margaret Thatcher. A visual representation of the female figure gives the allegory a concrete form that is lacking in literary examples. Yet the monuments Warner describes are by definition static, passive vehicles for the concepts they convey.

Allegorical figures like Britannia and Marianne were invented in order to embody the concept of their respective nations, and have no existence outside their allegorical roles. A few comparable allegorical representations of Scotland can be found prior to the twentieth century, named "Scotia" or "Scota", but given the lack of an established history or institutional significance for the Scottish figure, her pedigree is quite different from monumental figures such as Britannia in whose image she is constructed, especially since she appears almost entirely in literary form. Her very difference from the established figures she is supposed to emulate makes it obvious that the allegory is built upon a series of compelling but incompatible metaphors based on stereotypes of femininity: nation as virgin, nation as mother, nation as protectress, nation as victim. Close study of any female personification of Scotland demonstrates that the female figure cannot unproblematically represent a whole nation. Scotland's peculiar status as a nation highlights some of the problems of the woman-as-nation figure generally, and reveals some of the contradictions and inconsistencies inherent in the allegorical representation of the nation, making it necessarily multi-faceted and fragmentary. Chapter One considers these inconsistencies, looking particularly at the figure of Britannia, and surveys the few pre-twentieth-century examples of the allegory in Scotland, in the work of Robert Burns and others.

The first sustained use of various female figures to represent the Scottish nation was part of the political, linguistic and cultural revival known as the Scottish Literary Renaissance. Many of the literary incarnations of Scotland-as-woman, however, would be more properly called symbols than allegories since, particularly in the novels, they are psychologically realistic characters with secondary symbolic functions (see Frye 1971: 89). There is no unique Scotland-as-woman figure who functions as a symbol for this renaissance: rather, diverse authors associated with the movement created comparable female figures who may be read as symbolising the nation. The writers surveyed in Chapter Two all use the female figure in different ways, from Hugh MacDiarmid's "Gaelic muse" through Lewis Grassic Gibbon's much more down-to-earth "Chris Caledonia" to Naomi Mitchison's "Alba our mother". The image of Scotland-as-woman is dispersed, and this again highlights the figure's multiple connotations. The contradictions and inconsistencies are what make the twentieth-century Scotland-as-woman figure interesting. MacDiarmid describes the nation in his long poem *Direadh* (1974) as "our multiform, our infinite Scotland", and elsewhere as "a polyhedron he held in his brain, / Every side of it visible at once" (MacDiarmid 1985: 1170, 1070). His celebration of the plurality of Scotland, following on from Gregory Smith's description of the positive diversity of Scottish literature in *Scottish Literature: Character and Influence* (1919), provides a context in which to situate the multiple female personifications of Scotland. But Scottish literary critics have not always interpreted this multiplicity positively, and the female Scotland, as well as in some ways personifying the hopes of the Literary Renaissance, also seems to incarnate many anxieties about the nation.

Two particularly difficult aspects of the female personification of Scotland reflect problems in conceptions of Scotland generally: the female nation as victim and the female nation as monster. Both are explored brilliantly in two novels by Alasdair Gray, and also find echoes in other late twentieth-century writing. The female victim metaphor, used in order to evoke the necessity of defending the nation against external threats, is intrinsic to the basic model of woman-as-nation. In the Scottish context, however, this is associated with both the reiteration of cultural inferiority dubbed the "Scottish cringe" and a certain abdication of responsibility that leads to an acceptance of the inevitability of Scotland's political situation. Chapter Three focuses on Gray's ironising of the traps surrounding the construction of nation-woman-victim in his novel *1982, Janine* (1984). Chapter Four considers a problem more specific to Scotland: the image of the female nation as in some way deformed. The woman-as-nation model tends to emphasise the wholeness and goodness of the female form, but the angel stereotype of femininity always has the potential to mutate into its polar opposite, the female monster (Gilbert and Gubar:

1979: 17). Since, for political reasons, the woman-as-nation model
cannot work in the Scottish context, she is pulled in opposite
directions, thereby becoming monstrous, as illustrated by the work of
both Alasdair Gray and Liz Lochhead. This also has its echo in
twentieth-century critical approaches to Scotland, as Gregory Smith's
term "Caledonian antisyzygy" has been appropriated by later critics
and developed into a discourse of doubleness and schizophrenia to
describe Scotland – effectively making Scotland into a monster.


This book began as a study of the Scotland-as-woman figure, and has
ended up as an exploration of why such a figure is so difficult to
determine, and so problematic when she does appear. She also
functions as a symbol – a muse, even – for the heavily masculine
profile of Scottish literature in the twentieth century and before. The
woman-as-nation allegory requires that its citizens be male, and
Naomi Mitchison and Willa Muir's attempts, discussed in Chapter
Two, to fit into the Literary Renaissance's very masculine system of
myth, show to what extent woman as nation is a male allegory. The
final chapter considers various Scottish women writers of the 1990s
who have in different ways broken free from the constrictive constructions of women in Scottish literature, and the constrictions surrounding Scottish literature itself. The inheritance of the Scottish Renaissance means that Scottish literature still tends to be influenced by
masculine constructions of Scottishness, which are often reinforced by
a critical desire to categorise and define exactly what "Scottish literature" is. A close study of the problems surrounding the allegorical
Scotland-as-woman figure also reveals many problems with critical
assumptions about Scotland's culture and literature. Ellen Galford,
rather like Alasdair Gray, is able to mock both Scottish tradition and
the Scotland-as-woman figure, while A.L. Kennedy and Janice
Galloway in different ways evade or refuse the symbolic use of the
female body. The work of all these writers reveals the emptiness at the
core of the traditional representation of the nation in female form and
exemplifies a variety of possible ways to put Scottish women at the
centre of their own narratives.

# Chapter One

## Woman as Nation

Create oorsels, syne bairns, syne race.
Sae on the cod I see't in you
Wi' Maidenkirk to John o'Groats
The bosom that you draw me to. (MacDiarmid 1987: 78, ll.957–60)

Scotland has been fucked and I am one of the fuckers who fucked her. (Gray 1984: 136)

Hugh MacDiarmid's *A Drunk Man Looks at the Thistle* (1926) creates a kaleidoscopic, shape-shifting, and at times nightmarish vision of Scotland. In the course of the poem it becomes clear that the nation the Drunk Man contemplates is necessarily female. Sixty years later, Alasdair Gray revisits "the matter of Scotland refracted through alcoholic reverie" in *1982, Janine* (1984) and develops many of MacDiarmid's ideas, particularly his gendered vision of Scotland. MacDiarmid and Gray, at opposite ends of the twentieth century, both provide compelling, though unattractive, visions of Scotland as a nation. Both narrate the nation from the point of view of a disenchanted male citizen, who projects his anxieties and his hopes onto the feminised nation. In the quotation above, MacDiarmid's Drunk Man superimposes the female body onto the map of Scotland. The female body is sexualised, seen from above with her head lying on the pillow, associated with the production of "bairns", and with the borders of the nation, both ethnic and geographical. The female body potentially creates not only the race, but also the very borders of the nation, from Maidenkirk to John o'Groats. In *1982, Janine*, Gray picks up on the latent sexism in MacDiarmid's poem and turns it into explicit pornographic narrative. The main character, Jock, imagines a series of female fantasy figures, and the sexual exploitation of these women in his fantasies functions as a metaphor for colonial exploitation.

MacDiarmid and Gray both narrate the nation through the medium of the female body, and in so doing they are both drawing on a long history of representing the nation in female form. It is a particularly powerful allegory because it draws on a range of different traditions of representing the female body. Historically, the female form has been used to represent abstract virtues, such as justice, truth and beauty, due to their grammatical gender in most Indo-European languages (Warner 1996: xxi). This capacity of the female form to contain an abstraction contributes to the success of the nation-as-woman figure. But the female body is also associated with the land itself, both aesthetically and in metaphors of fertility. Thanks to these associations, the female body can represent both the physical, geographical existence of the nation, as in MacDiarmid's "from Maidenkirk to John o'Groats", and also the more abstract idea or essence of the nation, which is more difficult to illustrate.


**The aegis of Britannia**

The female personification of nation in the form of Britannia is, of course, familiar. With her helmet, breastplate and trident, she has appeared on coins and stamps, and in political cartoons. Although she does not carry quite the same institutional signification as the figure of Marianne, who appears on the façade of civic buildings throughout France (Agulhon 1979: 34), she is a recognisable symbol of Britishness, and has enjoyed a long and illustrious history. Britannia's past glories and her semi-institutional function combine to make her a stable and accepted personification of the British nation, and as such she hinders any development of a female figure representing Scotland. Britannia's history can be traced back to the reign of Elizabeth I of England, before Scotland and England were united by the Union of the Crowns. The "Ditchley Portrait" of Elizabeth I in the National Portrait Gallery, London (Marcus Gheeraerts the Younger, c.1592), shows Elizabeth standing on a map of the British Isles. Her feet are on Ditchley in Oxfordshire, and her full skirts are mirrored in the broad base of southern England. Elizabeth rises up from the map and her body replaces the shape of Britain. Although this portrait does not explicitly associate Elizabeth with Britannia, it illustrates precisely the problem that Britannia poses for any potential female personification of Scotland. She occupies the space that would be occupied by a Scotland-as-woman figure.

The cult that focussed on the figure of Elizabeth, the "Virgin Queen", during her reign, certainly contributed to the development of the Britannia figure, drawing as it did on classical mythology and also

displacing Marian iconography. The queen's virgin body, iconographically associated with the protection of England's national
boundaries, emphasised the importance of female chastity to national
integrity. The warlike defence of English territory during the reign of
Elizabeth, and particularly the defeat of the Spanish Armada in 1588,
provoked a revival of patriotic iconography, including the warlike
figure of Boadicea (or Boudicca), legendary Queen of the ancient
British tribe of the Iceni. Britannia inherited both Elizabeth's chastity
and Boadicea's warlike spirit (Samuel 1989: xxiii; Warner 1996: 49–
51). The earliest extant representation in the modern period of a figure
named "Britannia", however, appeared after the death of Elizabeth in
William Camden's *Britannia* (1607), in the reign of James VI of
Scotland and I of England. She also forms the frontispiece to Michael
Drayton's elaborately illustrated *Poly-Olbion* (1612–22), where she
sits in the centre of a triumphal arch. James's accession to the throne
of England in 1603 brought the two countries politically closer
together than they had been under Elizabeth, and James was keen on
the idea of further union between Scotland and England, since the two
countries were, in a sense, united in his body. He styled himself "King
of Great Britain", and is also credited with designing the Union flag.

Thus even before the political union of Scotland and England, a
Britannia figure was already reproducing the physical borders of the
entire island and embodying James's hope for the construction of a
British identity. And as she developed, she took on an increasingly
institutional role. In political cartoons of the eighteenth century she
primarily symbolised the British constitution and the rights of the
British people as enshrined in the law, but by the nineteenth century
she came more and more to symbolise the ruling power; the accession
of Queen Victoria naturally strengthened this association. The institutional function of the woman-as-nation figure is connected to but distinct from the more vague and romantic personification of the nation's
essence. The appearance of Britannia on coins and banknotes, stamps
and official documents, and her association with law and government,
make her part of the apparatus of the state. She represents not only the
nation's soul but also its institutional body. This institutional existence
is denied to a Scotland-as-woman figure because, since the Act of
Union in 1707, there has been no need to represent Scotland institutionally. The institutional use of Britannia – and also of Marianne in
France – was most popular in the nineteenth century, and certainly had

not begun before the eighteenth. There is thus no history of an institutional Scotland-as-woman figure prior to Union, and no possible role for one afterwards.

As Scotland is institutionally subsumed into the British state, we might expect it to be allegorically subsumed into the Britannia figure. Yet this does not work because of Scotland's peculiar political situation. While Scotland (at least until 1999) was entirely governed by the British parliament in Westminster, and thus logically under the aegis of Britannia, Scotland's identity as a nation (as distinct from its institutional identity) remained strong and clearly separate from its southern neighbour. To represent Scotland by Britannia would be unthinkable, particularly given the perennial problem that Britannia is often popularly associated with England rather than Britain. One might expect this rather unbalanced situation to complicate the figure of Britannia, but in fact she takes it in her stride, and the problems are all faced by the Scotland-as-woman figure, on the occasions when she does appear. The imbalance within the British Isles does not disrupt Britannia partly because it is overridden by one of the principal rules governing the allegory of the nation as a woman.

The allegorical female figure has to be whole, complete, an unbroken shell, in order to contain the virtue or essence that she embodies. This, as Marina Warner points out, is why emphasis is so often placed on the chastity of the symbolic female figure. Allegorical figures are able to function as closed, sealed containers because they are imagined to be sexually virtuous, chaste, "whole", unbroken and therefore able to hold concepts like water. To illustrate the qualities of the allegorical female figure, Warner tells the story of the Vestal Virgin Tuccia, who was accused of breaking her vow of chastity and, in order to prove that she was indeed chaste, miraculously managed to carry water in a sieve from the river (Warner 1996: 241–42). As she further illustrates, the bodies of allegorical female figures are often reinforced:

[…] either literally, when they are made of bronze, or metaphorically, when they are drawn, painted or described clad in armour. The content is the concept they contain, and the more securely they contain it, the more the content itself gains in fullness and sureness and definition and substance. (258)

In order properly to represent a strong Britain, then, the Britannia figure must have uncomplicated and impenetrable boundaries, and to acknowledge the complexities created by the position of Scotland would be to weaken those boundaries.

The boundaries of the nation-as-woman figure are doubly important. The emphasis on the reinforced outside of the allegorical figure increases the impression of her being a container who holds not only the essence of the nation but also its citizens. Marina Warner memorably illustrates this with her description of joining the millions of Americans who make the pilgrimage to climb up the inside of the Statue of Liberty. The hollow shell of the female nation surrounds and contains, literally incorporates, the many bodies of its citizens. As Warner puts it, "we can all live inside Britannia or Liberty's skin" (12). This symbolic reproduction of boundaries is then transposed onto the map, and the reinforced boundaries of the allegorical figure double as the borders of the nation itself. This is particularly visually satisfying in the case of Britannia, whose outline transfers without too much difficulty onto the very clearly defined borders of mainland Britain. She symbolises Britain iconographically, nominally and institutionally, and the fact that part of the island she embodies considers itself to be a nation in its own right does not trouble her sculptured features. (The location of first Ireland and later Northern Ireland within the composite figure of Britannia is yet another problem, and far too complex to treat here. Iconographically, if the body of Britannia reproduces more or less the shape of mainland Britain, her shield often appears in the place of Ireland.)

What becomes interesting when we study the way Scotland has been represented as a woman is how little the allegory has in fact been used, compared to established institutional figures such as Britannia as well as to the much stronger allegorical literary tradition in Ireland. As Christopher Harvie puts it, "Auld Scotia – who she?", going on to add, "Scotia not only isn't Britannia, she does not seem to be there at all" (Harvie 2002: 28). The relative absence of any Scotland-as-woman figure is striking. She can be found, if you look for her, but before the twentieth century it is difficult to come up with even a handful of examples of women representing Scotland. The unbroken shell of the nation-as-woman figure, reproducing the borders of the nation, causes problems for any such representation of Scotland, for the simple reason that Scotland's borders are not entirely clear or fixed. The political and institutional borders of the modern state are not the same as the geographical limits of the ancient nation. Ernest Gellner (1983: 1)

defines nationalism as "primarily a political principle, which holds
that the political and the national unit should be congruent", and it is
precisely this lack of correspondence between the borders of Scotland
as a nation and the boundaries of the political system to which Scotland belongs which complicates the woman-vessel-nation symbolism.
The lack of any institutional role for Scotland-as-woman post 1707
means that opportunities for the use of the figure have been restricted.
If she cannot represent an existing nation-state, she can only function
either as the incarnation of the ancient nation or as a mobilising symbol of oppositional nationalism. And if there is no institutional stage
on which she can appear, her appearances are limited to the literary.

**The landscape of home**

Stephen Daniels claims in *Fields of Vision* that "national identities are
co-ordinated, often largely defined, by 'legends and landscapes'"
(1993: 5). Literary constructions of Scotland, particularly in the period
of the Scottish Literary Renaissance in the early twentieth century,
tend to narrate their legends through landscapes. These landscapes are
predominantly rural, whether wild and untamed or rolling and agricultural. They are also often gendered landscapes, providing an important metaphor for the literary incarnations of Scotland which appear in the period. These personifications of Scotland do not appear on
town halls or on currency, and are not part of the institutional and
urban state apparatus, but rather are strongly associated with the land
itself, and a much more primordial conception of nation.

Landscape, in Daniels' definition, "gives visible shape" to the
imagined community of the nation (Daniels 1993: 5), and this is often
associated with the female shape of the personified nation. In Michael
Drayton's *Poly-Olbion* (1612) the figure of Britannia, again loosely
resembling the shape of the island and surrounded by sea, is clothed in
a cloak showing the British landscape, and bears in her arms a huge
shell filled with the fruits of the land. *Poly-Olbion*, a "topographical
poem", is itself an excellent example of a gendered landscape giving
shape to the nation, as each poem about a different county of England
is illustrated by a map crammed with images of towns and rivers
represented by tiny images of women, and hills topped by men
wearing hats. The female gendered landscape serves several purposes.

It allows us to locate the abstract personification of the nation in the specificity of a distinctive landscape, and connects it, as in the case of the *Poly-Olbion* image or the Ditchley portrait of Elizabeth I, with the geographical boundaries of the nation. However, the aesthetic parallel between the outward appearance of the female figure and the visible shape of the landscape develops easily into a parallel between the female body and the land itself, based not on aesthetic considerations but on their shared reproductive potential. The association of agricultural fertility with female fertility, already implicit in the fruit carried by the *Poly-Olbion* Britannia, provides a metaphor of the nation as a mother who both reproduces and nurtures.

In their collection of essays *Woman-Nation-State* (1989), Nira Yuval-Davis and Floya Anthias identify "reproduction", both biological and metaphorical, as the key term in defining the involvement of women in ethnic and national processes. They list five ways in which women may be involved:

1. as biological reproducers of members of ethnic collectivities
2. as reproducers of the boundaries of ethnic/national groups
3. participating centrally in the ideological reproduction of the collectivity and as transmitters of its culture
4. as signifiers of ethnic/national differences – as a focus and symbol in ideological discourses used in the construction, reproduction and transformation of ethnic/national categories
5. as participants in national, economic, political and military struggles. (Yuval-Davis and Anthias 1989: 7)

For Yuval-Davis and Anthias the female body reproduces the boundaries of the nation or ethnic group, biologically and ideologically. Their list deals predominantly with actual women rather than the symbolic woman as the personification of the nation, but many of their points illustrate how biological function overlaps with symbolic function, and together feed into the construction of the allegorical figure. In their list "woman" is equated with "mother", and therefore biological reproducer. This notion of biological reproduction is then transferred first to the reproduction of members of the race/nation and then to the symbolic reproduction of the boundaries of the nation. This symbolic reproduction is transferred to the reproduction of ideologies, generating the idea of the mother as the receptacle and transmitter of tradition and history. All these shifting forms of reproduction contribute to the construction of a single female figure representing the nation, a focus for discourses of national identity.

The metaphor of the motherland is powerful, and is rooted in the English language in the phrases "mother country" and "mother tongue". Benedict Anderson points out that familial and domestic metaphors provide many terms used to refer to the nation: motherland, *Vaterland, patria, Heimat* (Anderson 1991: 143). Anderson does not distinguish between paternal and maternal labels for the "homeland", but the figure of the mother provides a nexus of other associations which support the metaphor of the "motherland". The fascination with origins, national or otherwise, leads back to the body of the mother, and the association of nation with mother bolsters the belief in the nation as something to which we are "naturally" tied. The umbilical cord between nation and citizen both connects and nurtures, and the mother as the source not only of food but also of culture is another strand in the construction of the motherland metaphor. Parental metaphors of motherland or fatherland necessarily construct the nation as something anterior. According to this metaphor, the nation produces its citizens, rather than the other way around. Believing in the nation as a pre-existing entity relieves us of the responsibility of imagining the nation. Anderson makes a distinction between nation-states, which may be constructed as "new" and "historical", and nations, which always "loom out of an immemorial past" (11). The nation is thus outside the historical process. It cannot be something which we have created, it has to be something which created us, because otherwise we are alone and responsible. Thus the metaphorical nexus of mother, land and nation evokes something older than institutional incarnations of nation such as Marianne – *Blut und Boden* rather than the legal and political boundaries of the nation. "Nothing endures but the land", as Chris says in Lewis Grassic Gibbon's *Sunset Song* ([1932] 1995: 119); both the fertility and the permanence of the land are important to this metaphor. The land is at the same time organic and static; it both reproduces and continues to exist. Through this identification with the land, it is the sexualised and maternal female body which comes to embody the nation.

Walter Scott feminises the romantic Highland landscape in his *Lay of the Last Minstrel* (1805) as "O Caledonia! stern and wild, / Meet nurse for a poetic child!" (Scott 1899: 78). This is what Simon Schama describes as the "ferocious enchantment" of national identity described through landscape, "its topography mapped, elaborated, and enriched as a homeland" (Schama 1995: 15). Scott does not specify the gender of the poetic child thus enchanted, but Elspeth Barker in her novel *O Caledonia* (1991) illustrates clearly that his romantic female personification of the nation and its landscape only works if the poetic child is male. Scott indeed continues, "Land of my sires! what mortal hand / Can e'er untie the filial band, / That knits me to thy rugged strand!", which suggests a patrilinear vision of nationhood, while Caledonia, feminised, is in Scott's poem both mother and muse, nourishing her sons with inspiration from her native soil. In the words of Gillian Rose, there is "no place for women" in this landscape, when place becomes female (Rose 1993: 41). Women *are* the landscape, just as they *are* the nation, but they do not inhabit the landscape. When MacDiarmid superimposes the female body onto the map of Scotland "wi' Maidenkirk to John o'Groats", the poem continues: "And nae Scot wi' a wumman lies / But I am he…" (MacDiarmid 1987: 78, ll.961–62). As Christopher Whyte points out, the terms "Scot" and "wumman" are clearly polarised, since a Scot, in this definition, must be someone who sleeps with women. Thus women are excluded from the subject position "Scot" (Whyte 1995a: 30). While women are seen as receptacles of nationhood, they do not fully participate in that nationhood.

Alasdair Gray too follows a similar pattern, relating citizenship to male (heterosexual) sexuality. He proposes in *Why Scots Should Rule Scotland 1997* that "landscape is what defines most lasting nations" (Gray 1997: 1), and images of recognisably Scottish landscapes illustrate his fiction, as in the frontispieces to *Lanark* (1981) or the portrait of "Bella Caledonia" in *Poor Things* (1992a: 45). Bella's positioning in this portrait recalls the Mona Lisa, but the landscape in front of which she stands is recognisably Scottish, containing mountains and the Forth Rail Bridge. The composition of the portrait is such that the lines of Bella's body seem to be a continuation of the lines of the landscape behind her. This merging of the female body with the national landscape also occurs in Gray's second novel *1982, Janine*, in this passage where Jock describes his relationship to the female body:

Women's bodies do that for me when I am allowed to hold them and I stop being
nervous. I am not referring to fucking, I am referring to THE LANDSCAPE OF
HOME. Every woman has her own unique scale of proportions but the order of these
warm soft slopes and declivities is the same, and whenever I am allowed to explore
one of these landscapes I feel I have never been away from it. [...] the familiarity of
Denny's thighs, buttocks, stomach, glens, glades, banks and braes must have been
mine when I was born. (Gray 1984: 167)

The description of Denny's body here slides into a description of
landscape. Jock has already described every human body as a potential sexual landscape (48), but this landscape, as he himself indicates,
goes beyond the sexual. As the curves of Denny's body merge with
the landscape her individual body disappears; as the landscape over-
writes her body, she is effectively dehumanised. Jock's encounter with
her body becomes an encounter with something much larger, the
"landscape of home" which subsumes female bodies to its purposes.
The symbolic female body represents not an individual but a space.
Elsewhere in the novel, Jock describes his mother as "not a person but
the climate I grew up in" (50), evoking a sense of security and comfort
but at the same time dehumanising the mother. Just as Denny's body
merges with the landscape, so Jock's mother becomes something
larger than herself – no longer an individual but a space to be inhabited. The space created by the mother's body is extended to the com-
forting and maternal space of the home. The description of Denny's
body is also maternal: the "landscape of home" which "must have
been [his] when [he] was born" assimilates Denny to the maternal
body, to the motherland, and yet at the same time the land is a lover.
This comes close to what Annette Kolodny describes in *The Lay of the
Land* as

probably America's oldest and most cherished fantasy [...] an experience of the land
as essentially feminine – that is, not simply the land as mother, but the land as woman,
the total female principle of gratification – enclosing the individual in an environment
of receptivity, repose, and painless and integral satisfaction. (Kolodny 1975: 4)

Kolodny describes the complexity of the metaphor: the landscape is at
once maternal and sensual.
      Jock's innocent encounter with the national landscape in the
body of Denny is rewritten elsewhere in the book in the crudest terms:
"Scotland has been fucked and I am one of the fuckers who fucked
her" (Gray 1984: 136). This is the flip-side of the personification of

the nation as mother or lover: contained within the metaphor is the possibility of the desecration of that cherished body from without or from within. The iconography of home not only reinforces a sense of the nation as a place of belonging in a familial sense, it also characterises the nation as a space which may be attacked and must be protected. The female and maternal space of home must be defended against all external threats, and thus in wartime the metaphor of nation as home acquires extra significance. In the first year of the Second World War, the following British institutions were created: the Ministry of Home Security, the Home Secretary, the Home Guard, the Home Intelligence Unit and the BBC Home Service. In each case, as Antonia Lant points out, the word "home" is interchangeable with "national" (Lant 1996: 17).

This emphasis on defending the homeland is echoed in the costumes of Britannia and Marianne, who are both generally represented in armour, or at least as armed. Helvetia on Swiss coins clutches a spear and a shield, Britannia wears a helmet and full armour. Maurice Agulhon concludes his study of the figure of Marianne by suggesting that what she ultimately represents is the figure of the soldier, an iconography which can be traced back to Joan of Arc (1989: 349). Double meanings surround this martial imagery, because while the armoured woman as nation signifies that she is the defender of the nation, the rhetoric of woman as nation generally constructs her as someone to be defended. This double existence as both defender and defended is epitomised in the figure of the mother. The connotations of security provided by the calm, poised and governing figure of Britannia find their ultimate representation in the image of the home and the figure of the mother. Much of the doubleness surrounding the nation represented as a woman can be explained by the contradictions contained within the figure of the mother. She creates the safe space of home, and defends and protects her children; yet at the same time she is constructed as an iconic figure to be defended. Her construction depends upon the dual identification of the male nationalist figure: he is both the child created and defended by the powerful mother figure, and the man of action in defence of his country. The tasks of defending, and indeed of defining, the nation are seen as definitively male. As Yuval-Davis and Anthias point out in *Woman-Nation-State*, nationalist discourse makes much use of the allegory of "the nation as a loved woman in danger or as a mother who lost her sons in battle"

(1989: 9–10), but this gendered iconography casts only men as citizens, as the nationalist sons of the mother-nation.

This is, ultimately, the strangest paradox surrounding the female personification of the nation. While the female is elevated to the status of goddess, idealised and attributed virtues and qualities of the highest order, she is metaphorically excluded from participation in what Benedict Anderson calls the "deep, horizontal comradeship" of the nation, the "fraternity" which is by definition a male preserve (Anderson 1991: 7). The difference between male and female personifications of the nation, as Marina Warner points out, is that male icons such as John Bull, the personification of English character in literature and cartoons, often pictured wearing a Union Jack waistcoat, and his counterpart Uncle Sam in the United States, represent typical citizens of England and the States. The male symbol of nation is an individual, and often represents "the people", whereas female symbols of nation, such as Britannia or the Statue of Liberty, represent the nation as a whole in a more abstract way (Warner 1996: 12). Agulhon makes a similar distinction between Marianne, the generic, abstract symbol of France, and Napoleon, the individual male agent of history (Agulhon 1989: 40). Women are effectively disenfranchised from the vision of nation surrounding the female figurehead. Of course, many of these figureheads developed in periods when women did not share fundamental political rights with men, and so could not count as citizens in the strict definition of the term, even in Republican France (Landes 2001:4). But this is one more thing that makes the woman-as-nation figure obsolete in a modern society, and means that her appearance in twentieth-century Scottish literature is fraught with problems.

The classical simplicity of the Britannia or Helvetia figure hides a series of contradictions. As soon as we begin to unpack the metaphor and pursue the implications of the woman-as-nation figure, fault lines appear in the sculpted smoothness of her robes. The conflicting constructions of the nation as powerful progenetrix and damsel in distress both depend upon each other, and both are explicitly sexualised versions of the body of the woman as nation. To further complicate the allegory, as well as being defender and defended, she is also, necessarily, both sexual and asexual. Despite the sexuality written into the mother-nation and the lover-nation, she is also required to be chaste and virginal to provide a suitable vessel for her allegorical contents – and also to guarantee that the borders of the nation have not been penetrated by attack from outside. We move from the simplified and solitary image of the nation as a woman to a series of contradictory metaphors in which her very role demands that she be represented in interaction with others. Whether as mother, lover, virgin or whore, she is written into a narrative which places her in relation to the action of the nationalist male. The female figures representing Scotland that emerge in the twentieth century inherit these contradictions and flaws, but somehow fail to disguise them beneath a smooth façade in the way that Britannia does. Almost without exception, the figures of women symbolically representing Scotland pose some problem or other. All examples of woman-as-nation figures, from any nation, are problematic in similar ways, but in the Scottish context their flaws are highlighted by the curious political situation in which they are situated.

## "Anything you like": a confused history of the Scottish muse

The few Scotland-as-woman examples that we do find in Scottish literature prior to the twentieth century are complex in that they are not entirely Scottish – or not entirely symbols of nation: they seem somewhat hesitant about their iconic roles. This continues, of course, in the twentieth century. Given the lack of visibility of any Scotland-as-woman figure, though, it is curious how critics can go to some lengths to seek her out in order to illustrate that she arrives in the literature of the early twentieth century as part of an unbroken tradition, rather than being, on the contrary, determined by the precise historical moment. Hugh MacDiarmid, as we will see, attempts something similar when he claims to have found his "Gaelic muse" in the work of Thomas Carlyle (MacDiarmid [1943] 1972: 400). In "The Representation of Women in Scottish Literature", Douglas Dunn asserts:

Scotland, like the Muse, is a feminine term and Idea. Among the more obvious examples are Dame Scotia in *The Complaynt of Scotland*, Scota in Ross's *Helenore*, Burns's more local muse, Coila, in *The Vision*, and perhaps also Kilmeny in James Hogg. [...] It is an imaginative embodiment that leads to Chris Caledonia in Grassic Gibbon's novel. [...] Scotia can be dignified, proud, and lovely; she can be Queen Margaret, Mary, Queen of Scots, all the women in the songs and all the women who ever wrote them, sang them or heard them. She can be Kate, Mrs Tam O'Shanter [...] or the nimble daemon Nannie. [...] She can be anything you like. (Dunn 1994: 16–17)

This is worth quoting at length because Dunn offers a useful introduction to the way the nation-as-woman symbol has been used in Scottish
literature. At the same time, however, his critical approach exemplifies many of the problems associated with it. His article, as its title
implies, reassesses the representation of women throughout the history
of Scottish literature, from Barbour's *The Brus* to the present day.
This is a valuable project, and Dunn's general, if at times haphazard,
survey clears the way for more detailed analysis of the marked gender
bias of Scottish literature. Yet his identification of an omnipresent
female figure representing Scotland seems to be the result of a critical
need to impose a continuity of tradition upon Scottish literature. In
this instance it is not continuity in literature *per se* which concerns
him, but the continuity of the symbolic signifiers of national identity.
Dunn wants to read Scotland as woman as an unbroken tradition
stretching from the middle ages to the present day. However, his
"obvious examples" do no more than suggest a shadowy tradition
which does not stand up to close examination. He includes in his list
James Hogg's *Kilmeny*, but despite the poem's concerns with the past
and present state of Scotland, its heroine is neither explicitly nor
implicitly paralleled with the troubled nation, and its inclusion serves
rather to demonstrate the insubstantiality of the tradition which he
identifies.

Catherine Kerrigan also makes general and timeless statements
about the personification of Scotland as a woman. She describes how

[…] the idealised image of womanhood is personified as the symbol of the nation –
Caledonia – who represents order, community, continuity, stability, security, that is,
the collective values and purpose of the nation. (1994b: 107)

Kerrigan evokes "Caledonia" as if she was a household name. Yet the
Scotland-as-woman figure is insubstantial to the extent that she does
not even have one name that we can agree on. In Douglas Dunn's list
we have one Scotia and one Scota – none of the rest, apart from
Burns's "Coila", to whom I will return, even merit a national epithet.
As already mentioned, Walter Scott called "Caledonia" the "meet
nurse for a poetic child" in *The Lay of the Last Minstrel*, and Alasdair
Gray, in the twentieth century, chooses to play with the name
"Caledonia" in *Poor Things*. Burns also devotes one poem to
"Caledonia". And just to complicate matters, an anonymous
eighteenth-century poem apostrophises "Albania" (a Latin form of the

Gaelic Alba): "O loved Albania! hardy nurse of men!" (Gifford and Riach eds 2004: 82). But these are isolated occurrences. Neither Scotia nor Caledonia is widespread or well known enough to constitute a tradition of naming the female personification of the nation.

Yet part of the mythology of the woman-as-nation figure is that she has a long ancestry, just like the nation itself. As Catherine Kerrigan comments, the woman-as-nation figure can be read in parallel with the many "symbolic practices (legends, myths, flags, anthems, etc.)" which are part of the invented traditions of the nation (Kerrigan 1994a: 155; 1994b: 106; Hobsbawm and Ranger eds 1983: 1–14). Such traditions and artefacts are created in order to bolster a sense of national identity as natural and immemorial, and they are invested with an imagined history much longer than their actual history, in order to create an illusion of historical continuity. It is essential for the validity of the woman-as-nation tradition that she has always been there. Dunn uses "Tam O'Shanter" to suggest that Scotia may be "anything you like", from Tam's wife Kate to the "nimble daemon Nannie". Yet there is no suggestion in Burns' poem that either figure is intended to be read as anything of the kind. Dunn's "anything you like" avoids discussion of her embarrassing absences from the history of Scottish literature and epitomises the projection of a nation-as-woman figure onto the history of Scottish literature. This in itself is part of the twentieth-century construction of Scotland as a woman.

We have seen that the tradition of portraying the nation as a woman is not Scottish. It is a transnational tradition, and there are many established female figureheads of other nations with whom Scotia (or Caledonia) cannot compete. The tradition of the nation represented by a woman is often strengthened by links with other cultures. There is a crucial paradox in the construction of the figure in general: despite her status as an iconic figurehead of a single nation, she nevertheless seems to come from elsewhere. For example, the figure of Britannia which developed in the late eighteenth and early nineteenth centuries owed both her statuesque gravitas and her signature helmet to the influence of the Roman goddess Athena (Warner 1996: 47–48). The similarity of all these tall, stately, martial female icons, such as Britannia, Helvetia or Marianne, means that they all partake in a shared history of woman representing nation, each bolstering the credentials of the others. As Georg Kreis points out in his

discussion of the Helvetia figure, the representations of nations as
women vary as regards attributes and accessories, but not in type
(Kreis 1991: 21). Each woman is dressed in cultural specifics, such as
Marianne's red Phrygian cap representing the Republic and the
Revolution, and Britannia's breastplate and trident, but these are external to the basic model of nation as woman. The similarities between
the iconic figureheads are greater than their differences. Although
each figurehead is meant to embody a pure national essence, a shared
sisterhood seems more important than the distinct national identities
the individual women represent. This runs counter to the idea that the
woman-as-nation figure is home-grown, identified with the soil of her
native land – rather, she is part of a larger aristocratic family. In this
model the idea of nation itself is more important than individual
national identity, and this makes sense in the case of Scotland when
we consider that the use of a Scotland-as-woman figure asserts Scotland's similarity to other nations and her participation in the condition
of nationhood itself. Yet there is still a gap between the idea of the
nation-as-woman signifying "home" and the idea that she belongs to a
larger group external to the nation, and in various Scotland-as-woman
representations this is expressed by portraying her as in some way of
foreign origin.

The idea that the female nation type may be dressed in her culturally specific national identity is illustrated by the cloak of landscape
worn by the figure of Britannia in Michael Drayton's *Poly-Olbion*
(1612). Here again the native landscape is something in which the
female figure is dressed, rather than something with which she is
identified. Similar cloaks may be identified on two Scottish nation-as-
woman figures in Dunn's list. The "affligit lady dame scotia", as she
is described, of the sixteenth-century *Complaynt of Scotland*, appears
to the poet in a dream and he recounts the way in which she reprimands her three sons, the Three Estates, for the divisions which
threaten to destroy Scotland (Wedderburn [c.1550] 1979: 56). Dame
Scotia wears a mantle divided into three parts, engraved and embroi-
dered with images showing weapons and war; books, science and
charitable acts; and cattle and crops. Her mantle, however, is ragged
and torn, and the images faded and difficult to read (54–56). Scotia is
described in the poem as being "of excellent extraction and of ancient
genealogy", in keeping with the tradition of an immemorial ancestry,
but her pedigree may in fact be not so much Scottish as European, as

she has been identified as "modelled on [Alain] Chartier's 'France' who in turn is related to Boethius' 'Philosophy'" (Wedderburn 1979: xxxiii). This early allegorical personification of Scotland as a woman is seen to have continental and classical antecedents. With these credentials, Scotia is established in a textual tradition of female personification which is by no means limited to Scotland. She can claim an iconographic genealogy and membership of the larger family of iconic sisters, even while she wears the cloak which shows Scotland's former glory and present ruin.

Another culturally specific cloak occurs in Robert Burns's long poem "The Vision" written in 1784–85 (Burns 1969: 80–90). Here the poet, on the point of swearing an oath to give up poetry forever, is visited by a female figure whom he takes to be "some Scottish muse", due to the holly-boughs wrapped round her head and the "tartan sheen" of her dress. More important, though, is the description of her cloak, on which, as in Drayton's title page, the national landscape can be seen:

Her Mantle large, of greenish hue,
My gazing wonder chiefly drew;
Deep lights and shades, bold-mingling, threw
    A lustre grand;
And seemed, to my astonish'd view,
    A well-known Land. (ll.67–71)

In the eleven-stanza description of her cloak, with its rivers and mountains, and "ancient Borough" that rears her head from a "sandy valley" (ll.85–86), the details of the national landscape correspond closely to that worn by Drayton's Britannia, though the cloak of Burns's muse also resembles that of Dame Scotia in the *Complaynt* as it shows not only the landscape but also the people of Scotland and events in Scotland's history. These cloaks illustrate not only how territory may be mapped onto the female body, but also how the female body may be dressed in allegory, as if the identification of woman with the nation or the symbolic landscape was a cloak which could be put on, taken off, or even passed between different women.

However, Burns's muse complicates the model of nation as woman, for two reasons. Firstly, although the poet hails her as "some Scottish muse", she goes on to explain to him in detail that she is not the representation of Scotland, but only one of a large "aerial band" of

muses charged with looking after the Scottish people. She is only one
of the "lower orders" in charge of "humbler ranks of Human-kind"
including the "rustic bard". She is not Scotia – she is Coila, the representation of the district of Kyle in Ayrshire. As Ted Cowan and
Douglas Gifford point out, "it is significant that Burns, the National
Bard, in his 'The Vision', reduces Wedderburn's 'Dame Scotia' [...]
to 'Coila', a maiden embodiment of Kyle and Burns's native Ayrshire," remarking that with honourable exceptions, seventeenth and
eighteenth century Scottish poetry "withdraws from consideration of
the whole matter of Scotland" until the Scottish Renaissance (Cowan
and Gifford eds 1999: 6). Burns makes an extended allegorical use of
Scotland as a woman just once, in a poem titled "Caledonia" (1794)
(Burns 1979: 363–65), where Caledonia appears as an Amazon-like
warrior woman who battles with a series of allegorical enemy figures
including the "Anglian lion" and the "Scandinavian boar". The poem
finishes, rather bizarrely, by comparing Caledonia to the hypotenuse
of a right-angled triangle (ll.43–48)! Burns also briefly addresses
Scotia in the penultimate stanza of "The Cotter's Saturday Night'
(1785) (Burns 1979: 116–21): "O Scotia! My dear, my native soil! /
[...] Long may thy hardy sons of rustic toil / Be blessed with health
and peace and sweet content!" (ll.172–75).

Burns's failure to repeat the invocation of a national muse in the
much longer poem "The Vision" may suggest an uneasiness regarding
the personification of Scotland in female form. In all but name Coila
corresponds to many of the conventions and complexities of the muse
as nation, and this shift in focus from the national to the local highlights the way in which the Scottish muse is often rather out of focus,
unable to correspond entirely to the models of woman as nation that
are available for imitation. This out-of-focus quality is related to the
second way in which Coila complicates the nation-as-woman model.
For although she represents the local, there is a foreign quality to her:
on her first entrance she is described as "outlandish":

And by my ingle-lowe I saw,
    Now bleezan bright,
A tight, outlandish Hizzie, braw,
    Come full in sight. (ll.39–42)

Adjectives attesting to her physical attractiveness ("tight", "braw")
frame the central description of her: she is an *outlandish* Hizzie. Her

foreignness and otherness is framed by her attractiveness. The importance of the "well-known Land" illustrated on her cloak, and her role as muse to the "rustic bard" mean that she has this ambiguous quality of being both of the land and external to it. Strangely, woman both is the nation and comes from outside it.

This simultaneous elevation and exclusion of women becomes particularly significant when we consider Coila's purpose in visiting the rustic bard. She is not simply a personification of Kyle – she is a muse, who appears in order to dissuade the poet from swearing an oath that henceforth he would give up writing poetry. There is an overlap between the woman-as-nation figure and the poetic muse, which we see also in the prologue to Alexander Ross's "Helenore, or The Fortunate Shepherdess" (1778), where he invokes a muse named "Scota" (Ross [1778] 1938: 9–141). This figure functions for Ross as the poetic muse, as she jolts him from his despair that he will never write as well as Allan Ramsay by literally inspiring him to creation: "PUFF – I inspire you, sae you may begin" (1.51). However, she is also the incarnation of the nation, as her primary concern is that he should write in Scots rather than English. In case there should be any doubt regarding his conflation of the figures of muse and nation, in his invocation – "Say, Scota, that anes upon a day / Gar'd Allan Ramsay's hungry hert strings play"– "Scota" is footnoted with the helpful information "the name of my muse". Although Ross's text is not generally considered a major Scottish eighteenth-century work, his use of the muse figure as Scotland is revealing, if only because MacDiarmid goes on to combine the personification of the nation and the figure of the muse in a very similar way. Ross's muse becomes Scota at the intersection of literature and politics, or more specifically, at the point where language is used as both a literary and a political instrument. In Ross's prologue, Scota's injunction to the poet to write in her "ain leed" since we have "words a fouth, that we can ca' our ain" (ll.56–58) suggests the political potential of both language and literature as the expression of a sense of nationhood.

This overlap between woman-as-nation and muse is not a staple attribute of the woman-as-nation figure, and it is interesting that they combine in the Scottish context. Hugh MacDiarmid, too, as we shall see, makes great use of this overlap, particularly with his figure of the "Gaelic Muse". The long-established tradition of the female figure acting as muse, combined with the association of the female with the representation of abstract virtues, make it easy for the Scotland-as-woman figure to slip in to her apparently pre-ordained role, despite the shortage of models for the female personification of Scotland. The lack of an institutional role for a Scotland-as-woman figure means that literature becomes her natural habitat. Alexander Ross's muse Scota is very much concerned that he should write in Scots, and the production of literature in the national language is the most significant nationalist act to which she can push her sons.

But naturally, the implication of the figure of the female muse is that the poets will be her sons, and not her daughters. The model of nation that is established around the figure of the female nation, not only defines the role of citizen as male by default, but also the role of poet. The nation mothers the citizen; the muse more often acts as metaphorical lover to the poet, although in Burns's "The Vision", interestingly enough, Coila greets him "with an elder Sister's air" (l.137). Women are clearly excluded from this model of national literature: symbolically they do not belong to the nation and they cannot write about it either. As Robert Graves wrote in *The White Goddess* in 1948, "woman is not a poet: she is either a Muse or she is nothing." Although Graves goes on to qualify his claim – "this is not to say that a woman should refrain from writing poems; only, that she should write as a woman, not as if she were an honorary man" – it is clear that the consciously creative position of "poet" is defined as exclusively male (Graves [1948] 1961: 446–47). The term "muse" is implicated in this dynamic, that women inspire while men write. When the muse becomes confused with the female figure of the nation, it becomes doubly clear that there is no place for real women in this model of the nation, and no role for them to play outside the symbolic. Predictably enough, none of these scattered literary antecedents of the Scotland-as-woman figure prior to the twentieth century was the work of a female author. The conflation of the female nation and the female muse in the eighteenth century, however, already signals the problems created by the gendered vision of Scotland and Scottish literature which emerges in the twentieth century Scottish Renaissance.

# Chapter Two

## The Female Figure in the Scottish Renaissance

The painting "Poet's Pub" by Alexander Moffat (1980), although produced many years after the scene which it represents, functions as a powerful piece of iconography regarding the Scottish literary scene. A group of poets including Hugh MacDiarmid, Robert Garioch, Edwin Morgan, George Mackay Brown, and Norman MacCaig are gathered round a pub table, pints in hand, and in some cases pipes in mouth. The pub in question may be Milne's Bar in Edinburgh, as the history and mythology of the Scottish Renaissance identify it as the scene of many poetry- and whisky-fuelled evenings. The maleness of the assembled company is inescapable, and in it we may read the maleness of the Scottish literary community. There are no women in the foreground of the picture, but blurred and indistinct female figures may be distinguished, appropriately enough, on its margins. A female figure with long hair and bare arms slumps, her head propped up on her hand, at a table to the left of the group. At the door of the pub on the extreme right of the picture another indistinct woman leans against the doorpost. And towards the centre of the background of the picture is a roughly painted female figure dressed in what appears to be a Greek tunic which has slipped from her shoulders to expose her breasts. She is waving a Lion Rampant. Presumably this is the Scottish muse, her attentions somewhat divided on this particular occasion. She too is out of focus, a blur when compared to the crisp lines denoting the poets at their table, and although this may not have been to the forefront of the artist's mind, her blurred outline reveals the fuzzy contours which the nation's political situation forces upon its figurehead.

In the "Scottish Literary Renaissance" of the early twentieth century, we see for the first time something resembling a Scotland-as-woman figure shared among contemporary authors and texts. In the work of male writers such as Hugh MacDiarmid, Neil Gunn and Lewis Grassic Gibbon, a female figure linked to the Scottish land is very important. Although, as we have seen, there are instances of Scotland being represented as a woman in pre-twentieth century literature, they are fairly sparse and cannot be said to constitute a tradition as such, and there is certainly not a visual tradition of a Scotia or

Caledonia figure, as there is with Britannia or Helvetia. This lack of tradition means that we never have a very clear picture of who the Scottish muse, or the Scotland-as-woman figure might be, or what exactly she might look like, although there certainly seems to be a need for her to appear in the poems and novels of the 1920s and 1930s. The blurred outlines of the woman in the *Poet's Pub* picture, then, are oddly appropriate, as, given the lack of any established antecedents for the Scottish muse, or of any definite role for her to perform, she does tend to be rather indistinct.

Writers like MacDiarmid draw on the tradition of a female figure representing nation because it belongs to the stock iconography of nations. In order to assert Scotland's identity as a nation among other nations, Scotland must be represented by a female figurehead. However if the Scottish nation-as-woman figure is to represent the endurance and immemorial existence of the Scottish nation, as she does in the work of Gibbon, Gunn and MacDiarmid, the very tradition of using this figure must itself possess at least the illusion of an immemorial existence. MacDiarmid in particular is highly enamoured of the idea of an authentic Scottish muse who has been waiting for a suitably worthy poet to arrive and represent her again. The myth of the always already existing figure of the nation as a woman is very attractive since, as we have said, the mother nation *has* to have an anterior existence, because she exists outside the historical process and gives birth to the nation and its history. However, the lack of any significant Scottish tradition of nation as woman means that writers have to look elsewhere for models. Established and thoroughly institutionalised figures such as Britannia and Marianne provided one model, but closer to home and also more relevant to Scotland's political situation was the use of the nation-as-woman figure in the Irish Literary Revival, as in Yeats' play *Cathleen ni Houlihan* (1902).

The figure of Cathleen ni Houlihan is perhaps the finest example of a literary use of the nation-as-woman figure functioning as the inspiring genius of oppositional nationalism, and MacDiarmid explicitly acknowledges his appropriation of Yeats' figure in his poem "The Gaelic Muse" (1985: 660). In Yeats' play the eponymous figure appears as a poor old woman who has lost her "four beautiful green fields", and who travels the country in search of young men who are willing to fight and die for her. The devotion of these young men and their sacrifice for the mother country rejuvenates the poor old woman, and she becomes, in the last line of the play, "a young girl [with] the walk of a queen" (Yeats [1902] 1906: 15). The power of Yeats' symbolism in its contemporary context led Countess Markievicz to describe the play as "a kind of gospel", while the republican insurrectionist P. S. O'Hegarty found it "a sort of sacrament" (Kiberd 1996: 200). Yeats himself asked, in his 1939 poem "The Man and the Echo": "Did that play of mine send out / Certain men the English shot?" (Yeats 1968: 632).

The power of Yeats' image, however, was partly due to the fact that Ireland had a rich tradition of personifying the nation as a woman, from the pre-Christian sovereignty goddesses onwards. Figures of women in Mediaeval Irish literature that have been read as the personification of Ireland include Queen Medbh of Connacht, the tragic heroine Deirdre, and the Cailleac Bheara, an old hag who becomes young and beautiful again when she persuades a young man to make love to her, obviously the ancestor of Yeats' Cathleen ni Houlihan figure. From the seventeenth century onwards the Ireland-as-woman figure took on the role of embodying a suffering and oppressed nation, and appears under various names, including Roisín Dubh, the Sean Bhean Bhocht (the Poor Old Woman), and Caitlín ní Houlihán, who first appears as the personification of Ireland in the work of the Gaelic poet Heffernan in the late eighteenth century. In the genre of the *aisling*, a form of dream-vision poetry which developed in eighteenth century Ireland, the poet encounters a beautiful young woman, the *spéir-bhean*, or "sky-woman", who represents the spirit of Ireland, and who is waiting for the return of the exiled Jacobite pretender. The *spéir-bhean*, unlike the more ancient versions of Ireland as woman, is young and passive. Yeats' first use of the figure of Cathleen ni Houlihan, in the poem "Red Hanrahan's Song about Ireland" (Yeats 1968: 206–8), is very different from the Poor Old Woman of the play, and closer to the *spéir-bhean* of the *aisling* tradition (Johnson and Cairns eds 1991: 3–4; Cullingford 1993: 55–66).

The nineteenth century was the period in which the Britannia figure became really popular in the public imagination. Marianne in France and Helvetia in Switzerland also had their iconographic heydays in the late nineteenth century. Compared to these figures, there is a noticeable lack of Scotland-as-woman imagery in the nineteenth century, and no Scottish equivalent of Cathleen ni Houlihan. While the lack of institutional imagery can be explained by Scotland's lack of statehood, the fact that there is not even a figure of Scotland as a nationalist symbol may be linked less to the lack of an iconographic tradition than to what Tom Nairn refers to as Scotland's lack of any demonstrable nationalist consciousness throughout that period (Nairn 1981: 135). It is only in the early twentieth century that a number of similar versions of the allegory occur, and it seems logical to connect this with the emergence of nationalist politics in Scotland.

The appearance of a Scotland-as-woman figure can thus be linked directly to the "Scottish Renaissance", the political and cultural revival of the interwar period in Scotland. The various writers of the Scottish Renaissance were all (in their different ways) committed to creating a new mythology for Scotland, and in doing so they all sought in some way to redefine "home". Lewis Grassic Gibbon's historicisation of Scotland; Hugh MacDiarmid's a-historical re-appropriation of a patchwork of myth to recreate Scotland; Neil Gunn's epic treatment of Scotland, his emphasis on the journey and the sea: all these depend on the central creation of a myth of home. Although all three writers extended their grasp geographically, historically and mythologically beyond their own nation in order to define Scotland as it had not been defined before, still there needs to be a centre, a core which is "home" to which Gunn's epic traveller may return, to which MacDiarmid may introduce the elements of other cultures he makes relevant to Scotland. For each of these writers, this core is provided by the symbolic body of a woman. The quest for some kind of national authenticity led to a desire to locate "natural" national identity in the "natural" habitat of gender roles.

The various female figures representing Scotland during the early Scottish Renaissance depend very strongly on their reproductive potential, and on the metaphorical connection between the female body and the land. They provide stability for the nation which is being constructed and function as the guardians of the traditions of the ancient nation. But at the same time the job of constructing the nation is seen as predominantly male, and the virility of the Scottish race and the Scottish poet is emphasised. The "Poet's Pub" painting illustrates this theme of virility and Scottish poetry, which is particularly strong in criticism of the period of the Scottish Literary Renaissance. Kurt Wittig's *The Scottish Tradition in Literature* (1958) considers no women at all in his chapter "The Modern Makars" dealing with the poetry of the Renaissance. The reference Wittig's title makes to the mediaeval poets echoes MacDiarmid's chosen filiation with William Dunbar, and Wittig locates Marion Angus, Violet Jacob and Helen Cruickshank in the previous chapter, perhaps to avoid spoiling the perfect line of his sketch of the male makars. Wittig gives extended consideration to six men in his poetry chapter (Hugh MacDiarmid, William Soutar, Sydney Goodsir Smith, Douglas Young, Edwin Muir and George Bruce), and to three men in his chapter on "The Modern Novel": Eric Linklater, Lewis Grassic Gibbon and Neil Gunn, although to give him credit he does mention Naomi Mitchison's *The Bull Calves* and Dot Allan's *The Deans* (1929) and *Hunger March* (1931).

While the exclusion of women from the canon of mainstream literary movements is by no means exclusive to Scotland, the nationalist impulse of the Scottish Literary Renaissance movement may well have contributed to the highly virile profile of its dramatis personae. Marilyn Reizbaum suggests that the emphasis on virility in nationalist discourse in Scotland and also in Ireland during the same period may be "a response to the historical figuration of cultural 'inferiority' in stereotypes of the feminine" (Reizbaum 1992: 172). Scott's reinvention of an essentially Celtic Scotland is followed in the late nineteenth century by a tendency to theorise the Celtic race and Celtic literature as essentially feminine, in books such as Matthew Arnold's *The Study of Celtic Literature* (1867) and Ernest Renan's *La Poésie des Races Celtiques* (1860). The "inferiorism" experienced by Scotland is complicated by a discourse of feminisation and countered by the insistence on the virility of the Scottish Renaissance group. In Scotland this rejection of the feminine had one other specific "domestic" literary tradition on which to focus. Carol Anderson and Glenda Norquay suggest that the nostalgic and sentimental "Kailyard" novel represented a domesticity and parochialism from which the writers of the Scottish Renaissance felt the need to distance themselves (Anderson and Norquay 1984: 8). The "confident intellectual basis" (Dickson 1987a: 59) of MacDiarmid and other writers of the Renaissance regarding the validity and indeed existence of a Scottish identity and literary tradition was a stimulus towards creativity and imagination and represented a clear rejection of the "domesticity" of the Kailyard. But this rejection of domesticity is related to the process of creativity and not necessarily to subject matter. The domestic female

in the text becomes a necessary corollary to the virile profile of the
Renaissance poets.

The fact that the pantheon of the Scottish Renaissance has until
some recent re-evaluations been almost entirely male may be related
to the wider literary phenomenon of gendered canon formations.
Although there were undoubtedly more successful male than female
writers in the period, literary criticism is now beginning to uncover
and reintegrate the female writers who were active in the period. The
obligatory critical footnote mentioning Violet Jacob, Marion Angus
and Helen Cruickshank is beginning to be expanded into the text;
Willa Muir is being given critical recognition outwith her role as the
wife of Edwin; and Naomi Mitchison, Catherine Carswell and others
are now being written into the history of the Renaissance. Naomi
Mitchison and Willa Muir both engage with the figure of a woman
representing the nation, but both of them, precisely because of their
status as woman writers, highlight the problems surrounding the allegory. The female nation-figures created by male writers all display
flaws of some kind, which can be related at least in part to the dissonance between the traditional use of the body as a metaphor for the
state and Scotland's political position. Mitchison and Muir, however,
both try to identify themselves as Scottish writers with the female
figurehead of nation, and discover that this identification is not possible within the logic of the allegory.


## MacDiarmid's other women

Hugh MacDiarmid's use of a female figure to represent Scotland is
particular in that, in the 1920s at least, she is split straight down the
middle. MacDiarmid draws upon two distinct and opposed images of
women: the first earthly, domestic and physical; the second mysterious, alien and spiritual. In his later work, MacDiarmid's images of
women, such as the "Gaelic muse" or "Audh the deep-minded", are
more whole, although they are both more spiritual than physical beings. In his early work, however, many of MacDiarmid's anxieties
regarding language and nation are embedded in the representational
gap between "real" and ethereal women.

From his earliest poems there is a dual quality to MacDiarmid's
use of the female figure as personification of place or nation. In the

poems "Spanish Girl" and "La Belle Terre Sans Merci" he uses images of women to describe his experiences in Salonika with the Royal Army Medical Corps in 1916–18 (MacDiarmid 1985: 10–13; 1197–99). Most significant, however, is his use of the female figure in his long poem *A Drunk Man Looks at the Thistle* (1926), where the domestic yet absent figure of the Drunk Man's wife Jean is superimposed upon the map of Scotland. She is opposed, however, to another supernatural, shape-shifting and foreign muse figure, who complements Jean's earthy sexuality and association with home.

The figure of Jean is first mentioned in line 101 of *A Drunk Man* (MacDiarmid 1987) and it is her (projected) words which close the poem. She thus provides a thematic framing device for her husband's drunken moonlit contemplation of a thistle and his unfocused mental wanderings. No matter how far adrift the Drunk Man finds himself, the mention of Jean and memories of her body and their sex life function as a textual home, a point of reference to which the Drunk Man regularly returns. The figure of Jean in the poem is rooted in the physical, and in the descriptions of her we find an explicit account of physical sexuality which we do not see in the (albeit sensual) descriptions of the more mysterious and ethereal "silken leddy". In her role as the Drunk Man's wife, Jean functions as a symbolic constant in a poem where every other symbol undergoes a series of changes and acquires dark and nightmarish aspects. This constancy, her association with home and her connection to an earthy and familiar sexuality contribute to the image of her naked body on the bed as the map of Scotland, "wi Maidenkirk to John o'Groats" (1.959).

Jean is firmly located at home, occupying the same dramatic space as Tam O'Shanter's wife Kate, a fixed point to which the Drunk Man must eventually return. On his way home Tam encounters the "other" in the form of the witches' coven and the figure of the young witch Nannie in her "cutty sark". But rather than *Tam O'Shanter*'s brownies and bogles the Drunk Man experiences otherness in a more textual form, in a series of encounters with European philosophy and literature. While Jean is located at home and associated with the physical, the "silken leddy", the other side of the female coin, has no fixed abode, and her reappearance in different translations links her to the disconnectedness of the Drunk Man's cerebral journey.

The figure identified as the "silken leddy" appears only three times in the 2685 lines of *A Drunk Man*, and each appearance is in a translation, two from the Russian poet Alexander Blok and one "suggested by the German of" Else Lasker-Schüler. She is far less rooted in reality than the figure of Jean, and as each appearance associates her with alcohol, the supernatural or the moon, her very existence is in question. Yet her status as a symbol of woman within the poem, a counterpoint to the physical and safe version of femininity provided by Jean, makes her a very important figure, and her "otherness" throws new light on MacDiarmid's entire project.

The first appearance of the "silken leddy" in *A Drunk Man* is in a translation from Blok (ll.169–220). She is closely associated with the fluid and unstable symbols of alcohol and the moon, and may, it is suggested, be a vision of the Drunk Man himself, "transmuted by the mellow liquor" (ll.225–26). While the original Blok poem is clearly a description of a prostitute, MacDiarmid's translation includes no references which make this evident. And for Blok's title, translated as "The Lady Unknown", MacDiarmid substitutes "Poet's Pub", linking both the female figure and the transmuting liquor to the idea of creativity. The appearance of the lady serves to stimulate the Drunk Man to poetic activity and deeper thought. Her second appearance, which closely follows the first, is a "free adaptation" of another Blok poem which hails the arrival of a strange and unknown woman. Blok's poem is called "The Unknown Woman" but MacDiarmid changes this to "The Unknown Goddess", elevating the image of the woman to a protective and superior status. For the section immediately following this MacDiarmid supplies the title "My Nation's Soul" which suggests to Kenneth Buthlay that this goddess is "a Scottish deity, whom [MacDiarmid] suspects of trapping the Drunk Man in a particularly Scottish form of constricted religious morality" (MacDiarmid 1987: 25). (The division of *A Drunk Man* into 59 titled sections was for its inclusion in the 1962 *Collected Poems* [London: Macmillan, 1962]. Kenneth Buthlay's edition of the text discusses the history of this in detail [MacDiarmid 1987: xxxiv–vii]. Since the titles were evidently supplied by MacDiarmid they may be used to cast some light on readings of the poem, but as they were supplied 30 years after its composition they are perhaps not very much help in deducing MacDiarmid's original intentions).

Although Buthlay makes this connection, it seems to me important to note that at no point is the figure of the "silken leddy" explicitly related to nation or to Scotland. Indeed, the crucial thing about her is that she is *strange*, both in the supernatural nature of her appearances and in the fact that each of her appearances is in a translation, a "foreign" text. The strangeness of the "Unknown Goddess" – "The features lang forekent … are unforecast" (1.248) – implies that the familiar has been supplanted by something else. She is "fremt", she is "unkent", and she is opposed to the figure of Jean, whose body preserves the space of home and of nation. While Jean is associated with Scotland in a very physical way, the "silken leddy" comes from elsewhere.

MacDiarmid thus uses the female figure to represent both home and other, and introduces a dynamic of sexual jealousy to describe his cross-cultural influences. In the first Blok poem, the appearance of the "silken leddy" is preceded by a line in parentheses which is not from Blok: "Jean ettles nocht of this, puir lass" (1.186). This line is ambiguously placed and so it may merely be the drinking of which Jean is ignorant and not necessarily the contact with the mysterious woman. The very appearance of Jean in this section of the poem, however, serves to juxtapose the two female figures and to suggest the possibility of sexual infidelity. The Drunk Man finds himself caught between the forces of familiarity, physicality and home, represented by Jean, and the attractive, disruptive and foreign "other" woman. The disruption she causes is the same disruption caused by MacDiarmid's eclectic assimilation of foreign literatures and philosophies within a poem which claims to be looking at "the thistle".

In "Towards a New Scotland", in the collection *Stony Limits* (1934), MacDiarmid explicitly constructs his attraction to other literatures as a form of infidelity, addressing Scotland: "Ah, Scotland, you ken best. […] Yet gladly I rejected ither literatures for yours, / Nor covet them noo you've ootcast!" (MacDiarmid 1985: 452). Foreign, "ither" literature is set in the context of sexual jealousy, rejection and covetousness. This attraction to the other complicates and darkens the representation of Scotland, most particularly in the poem "Ode to all Rebels" where MacDiarmid envisages himself singing the praise of Scotland in a mixture of contempt and ecstasy:

As who, in love's embrace,
Forgetfully may frame
Above the poor slut's face
Another woman's name. (MacDiarmid 1985: 489)

Here again we are confronted with Scotland as a woman, in another pillow scene. But compared to the Drunk Man's image of the female form projected onto the map of Scotland, things seem to have gone rather wrong here. Scotland receives the poet's embraces, but she is the "poor slut" who stands in for another, unattainable figure. The association of the female personification of Scotland with physicality and the landscape acquires a more negative connotation. MacDiarmid's disenchantment with Scotland is projected sexually onto the female form. This disenchantment reaches its most bizarre realisation in Part II of the poem "Tarras", entitled "Why I Became a Scots Nationalist", in *Scots Unbound and Other Poems* (1932). Here the feminised harshness of the landscape is transferred onto the body of a woman representing Scotland, and the process of stimulating nationalism, of engaging with the nation, is described in explicitly sexual terms. The poetic voice explains that he does not want a "quick-fire cratur' / Wha hurries up the ways o' natur'", but rather, is happy

… when after lang and sair
Pursuit you yield yoursel' to me,
But wi' nae rapture, cauldly there,
Open but glowerin' callously,
Yet slow but surely heat until
You catch my flame against your will
And the mureburn tak's the hill. (MacDiarmid 1985: 339)

In this bizarre allegory, the description of a reluctant woman being coaxed to orgasm represents not so much the physical form of the nation but more the political consciousness of the Scottish people, and the sexual act becomes the slow progress of nationalist conviction. The climax is worth it, the poem seems to suggest, but the slow and raptureless process is a far cry from the joyous celebration of the body of Jean and the map of Scotland in *A Drunk Man*.

In his later poetry MacDiarmid fuses his two different female types: the physical, "real" woman represented by Jean, and the spiritual, ethereal type of the "silken leddy". In the figure of the "Gaelic Muse" these two very distinct constructions of femininity become merged into one governing female ideal, but MacDiarmid's practice of drawing on extra-Scottish sources for his muse continues. He highlights his habit of borrowing from other texts and cultures by using, as Peter McCarey points out, "about twenty names from a dozen different cultures" corresponding to his vision of the Gaelic muse (McCarey 1987: 124). The figure of Audh "the deep-minded", who is associated with MacDiarmid's later "poetry of knowledge", is drawn from the Norse sagas. But in the poetry surrounding his "Gaelic idea", MacDiarmid deliberately draws on the Irish tradition, and finds the female figure which he calls the "Brightness of Brightness" or the "Gaelic Muse" in the genre of the *aisling* where Yeats found inspiration for his Cathleen ni Houlihan. More specifically, MacDiarmid draws on the famous *aisling "Gile na Gile"* ["Brightness of Brightness"] by the late seventeenth- and early eighteenth-century Irish Gaelic poet Aodhagan O'Rathaille – which is included in Daniel Corkery's *Hidden Ireland*, often cited by MacDiarmid as one of his sources (Corkery [1924] 1967: 175–77). O'Rathaille's *spéir-bhean* is changed by MacDiarmid from the spirit of Ireland to the spirit of Scotland, or rather, to a Celtic spirit who is more Scottish than anything else. She incarnates MacDiarmid's "Gaelic Idea" and one fragment from O'Rathaille's vision poem is repeated in varying forms three times in three different poems, most significantly in "The Gaelic Muse" (see Stirling 2003: 111–14).

The first published version of "The Gaelic Muse", in MacDiarmid's autobiography *Lucky Poet* (1943), immediately follows his positive assessment of the Gaelic poets Sorley MacLean and George Campbell Hay. In their work MacDiarmid identifies the beginning of a Gaelic renaissance and the emergence of a Gaelic muse. He envisages this Gaelic renaissance as the logical development of his own Scots renaissance, though his own contribution to it is limited to a commentary and the insertion of Gaelic lexis into his poems. He claims to see the lady of MacLean's *Dàin do Eimhir* (1943) as yet another representation of "the Scottish muse", and draws on the poet O'Rathaille to apostrophise her:

At last, at last, I see her again
    In our long-lifeless glen,
Eidolon of our fallen race,
Shining in full renascent grace,
She whose hair is plaited
Like the generations of men,
And for whom my heart has waited
    Time out of ken. (MacDiarmid 1985: 657)

And yet this Scottish muse is represented by an Irish sovereignty goddess, rather as the "Vision of Scotland" in MacDiarmid's poem of the
same name "throws her headsquare off" to reveal "a mass / Of
authentic flaxen hair [...] Fine spun as newly-retted fibres / On a
sunlit Irish bleaching field" (MacDiarmid 1985: 1096). This vision of
Scotland is both "authentic" and "Irish". And Ireland indeed provides
a kind of authenticity for MacDiarmid in his construction of muses. In
"Towards a Celtic Front" (1953), he discusses Daniel Corkery's idea
that the Irish Gaelic tradition is an equivalent to the classical tradition
on which Western civilisation was founded. Quotations from classical
authors parallel references to Irish authors (MacDiarmid 1969b: 173).
The "Gaelic Idea" can thus draw on a different classical tradition.

Yet despite the cultural link between Scottish and Irish Gaelic
cultures crucial to MacDiarmid's pan-Celtic vision of the "Gaelic
idea", in "The Gaelic Muse" the *spéir-bhean* from the *aisling* and a
series of other Irish women clearly need to be imported into the Scottish tradition by the use of the appropriating and inclusive "our":

our Scottish *Gile na Gile* – [...]
our Sheila ní Gadhra,
Our Cathleen ní Houlihán, our *Druimfhionn Donn*,
Our *pé' n Éireinn í*, 'whoe'er she be'... (MacDiarmid 1985: 660)

MacDiarmid has already said "Deirdre, Audh – she has many names, /
But only one function" (MacDiarmid 1985: 658). He envisages his
muse as a unitary figure made up of many parts, a governing female
principle which subsumes many female figures, roles and names. In
addition to the Irish list, he invokes a series of Greek names which
describe different types of images of the Virgin Mary in Byzantine art:

Phaneromene,
Hodegetria, Chryseleusa,
Chrysopantanasa – Golden-universal Queen –
Pantiglykofilusa, Zoodotospygi (MacDiarmid 1985: 658)

Including these unfamiliar, polysyllabic appellations of the Virgin
Mary (which MacDiarmid glosses in footnotes) increases the strangeness of the text and the figure he is describing, and makes a veiled
reference to an established iconography of the female figure.

The eclectic provenance of the many names of the muse figure
points to the plurality of MacDiarmid's vision. But he faces a problem

in that the multi-cultural names of his muse highlight the fact that he is forced to draw on foreign models of the muse due to the lack of any Scottish literary precedents of the figure. The paradox of MacDiarmid's construction is that while he hails Sorley MacLean's *Dain do Eimhir* as symbolic of the return of the Gaelic muse to a land which has long been lacking her, he nonetheless needs to construct for her a convincing and at least partially Scottish genealogy. He finds in Thomas Carlyle's novel *Sartor Resartus* a vision and a phrase which attracts him (acknowledging his source in *Lucky Poet* ([1943] 1972: 400), although in later versions of "The Gaelic Muse" it goes unannotated):

The actual Air-Maiden once more we see,
Incorporated tangibility and reality,
Whose electric glance has thrilled the Gaels
Since time beyond memory. (MacDiarmid 1985: 658)

Carlyle's "actual Air-maiden, incorporated into tangibility and reality" (MacDiarmid slightly misquotes) is indeed particularly apposite to MacDiarmid's vision of his muse, as it unites the physical and the spiritual paradigms of femininity. The relevant passage from *Sartor Resartus* is as follows:

Thus was the young man, if all-sceptical of Demons and Angels such as the vulgar had once believed in, nevertheless not unvisited by hosts of true Sky-born, who visibly and audibly hovered around him wheresoever he went; and they had that religious worship in his thought, though as yet it was by their mere earthly and trivial name that he named them. But now, if on a soul so circumstanced, some actual Air-maiden, incorporated into tangibility and reality, should cast any electric glance of kind eyes, saying thereby, "Thou too mayst love and be loved"; and so kindle him, – good Heaven, what a volcanic, earthquake-bringing, all consuming fire were probably kindled! (Carlyle [1831] 1987: 104–5)

The terms "Air-maiden" and "Sky-born" are uncannily close to the *spéir-bhean* (sky-woman). Carlyle's passage makes no mention of the Gaels: the "electric glance" cast by the Air-maiden is a development of the description of love in terms of "universal Spiritual electricity". The extended metaphor of women as insubstantial and ethereal creatures – "all of air they were, all Soul and Form" – in Carlyle's novel is satirical at the expense of the character who thus describes them. However, by paralleling the Carlyle quotation with the fragment of

O'Rathaille's *Gile na Gile*, MacDiarmid attempts to construct the impression that the Gaelic muse he describes, combining the physical and the ethereal, can be found in the work of the greatest Scottish writers and thus can be truly claimed as a Scottish muse.

MacDiarmid's "Gaelic Muse" is stitched together from a range of sources to create an image of the eternal feminine. In his later poetry MacDiarmid complicates the recipe still further when he introduces the figure of "Audh, the deep-minded", drawn from Norse mythology. Like the "silken leddy", Audh first appears, in *Lucky Poet*, in a translation – this time of Rilke – in a poem which continues the echoes of classical mythology, as its description of a goddess being born from the sea very much resembles the story of the birth of Aphrodite or Venus. She develops to become a more mature version of the Scottish muse, valued primarily for her fertility: "Audh the Deep-Minded, wife and mother of chieftains Gaelic and Scandinavian..." (MacDiarmid [1943] 1972: 387).

All MacDiarmid's muse figures have literary pedigrees, and are textual muses before they are muses of nation or inspiration. They arrive in MacDiarmid's work from elsewhere, just as the "Young Audh" is born, Aphrodite-like, from the waves. He highlights their strangeness by his acknowledgement of all the original sources and languages from which he has drawn them, and they retain some element of that strangeness. They are translated into Scottish muses and adapted to MacDiarmid's purposes, but they are never fully assimilated into their new context, and remain slightly awkward in their new roles. The woman representing nation, as discussed by Marina Warner, is supposed to be whole, closed, limited. She represents one thing, the nation, and her wholeness reproduces the wholeness and the impermeability of the borders of the nation. MacDiarmid's muses are not whole, not one. They are multiple, and with their sources in multiple cultures and multiple texts they transgress borders and resist categorisation.

## Spirits of Place: Lewis Grassic Gibbon and Neil Gunn

MacDiarmid never creates – and perhaps doesn't want to create – a whole and unified female figure representing Scotland. His woman-as-Scotland figures are always complicated by competing constructions of femininity – or competing constructions of Scottishness – and yet this play of opposites is characteristic of his work generally. Lewis Grassic Gibbon creates a more down-to-earth female Scotland in the person of Chris Guthrie, who, in her identification with the land, is similar to the figure of Jean in MacDiarmid's *Drunk Man*. However the representation of Chris is also complicated by other considerations. MacDiarmid's poetry can accommodate his shape-shifting, changeable female figures, but Gibbon's trilogy *A Scots Quair*, because of its novel form, requires a psychologically coherent central character. Chris Guthrie's symbolic role sits uneasily with the narrative of the novel.

The explicit identification of Chris with the nation is made only twice in *A Scots Quair*, both times in *Cloud Howe*, the second book of the trilogy. The status of Chris as "Chris Caledonia" owes almost as much to subsequent critics of the novels as to Gibbon. The acceptance of Chris as Scotland by readers and critics says as much about the need for a Scotland-as-woman figurehead in the Renaissance as it does about the intentions of the authors of the period. Christopher Harvie suggests that Chris Guthrie, in the guise of "Chris Caledonia", acts as the "emotional 'point of rest'" for most Scots readers of *A Scots Quair* (Harvie 1991: 43). For Christopher Whyte, "Chris Guthrie functions as Chris Caledonia again and again in Gibbon's trilogy" (1995a: 31), while Thomas Richardson describes her as "the Scottish national metaphor" (1989: 127). Yet the actual instances of Chris being equated with Scotland do little to suggest such a heavy interpretation. In *Cloud Howe*, Chris's second husband, Robert Colquhoun, famously exclaims "Oh Chris Caledonia, I've married a nation!", while the new laird, Stephen Mowat, "felt he was stared at by Scotland herself" (Gibbon [1933] 1995: 139; 105). Kurt Wittig suggests a schematic reading of the trilogy whereby this identification may be expanded throughout the trilogy and throughout the span of Chris's life: "Chris, the woman, becomes, more and more 'Chris Caledonia'". She "comes from the land", her marriage to the Highlander Ewan Tavendale signifies the union of Highlands and Lowlands, and her second husband, the Rev. Robert Colquhoun, represents the ties that bind state and religion in Scotland (Wittig 1958: 331).

Various critics, engaging with Wittig's claims, have attributed the phrase "Scotland herself" to Wittig, though in fact he takes it from *Cloud Howe* (Hagemann 1991: 189; Murray 1987: 109). His reading

has been disputed on the grounds of Gibbon's own anti-nationalist
sentiments, and the otherwise proto-feminist treatment of women in
the trilogy as a whole (Hagemann 1991: 189; Dixon 1990: 289–301;
Burton 1984: 35–46). Gibbon's treatment of the question of reproductive rights – the suicide of Chris's mother on finding herself pregnant
again, and Chae Strachan's statement to his daughter that "life came
out of women through tunnels of pain and if God had planned women
for anything else but the bearing of children it was surely the saving of
them" (Gibbon [1932] 1995: 45) – speaks to a modern and sympa-
thetic attitude to women.

Such psychological realism co-exists uneasily with the symbolic
aspect of the character of Chris Guthrie. While explicit reference to
Chris as nation is made only twice, the identification of Chris with the
land is more sustained, though most exploited in the first book of the
trilogy, *Sunset Song*. Gibbon's feminisation of the agricultural landscape allows him to exploit the sexual metaphors implicit in the allegory, paralleling female and arable fertility and thus placing women in
a passive and receptive sexual role. In his short story "Clay", this
theme is expressed through his male protagonist's obsession with the
land. He describes his fields "as though they were women you'd to
prig and to pat afore they'd come on", and tends the land day and
night until the local people joke "that he'd take it to bed with him if he
could" (Gibbon [1934] 1967: 21; 23). Chris's relationship with the
land is more complex, as it is through her consciousness that we see
the land as an extension of herself and a means of expressing both her
sexual and her psychological identity. The four agriculturally titled
parts of *Sunset Song* ("Ploughing", "Drilling", "Seed-Time" and
"Harvest") correspond to stages in Chris's sexual and emotional development, giving structural support to the analogy of agriculture to
sexual reproduction and to the sexual act itself. These part-headings
are given further textual support. Chris as a young girl is described as
"no more than ploughed land still" (Gibbon [1946] 1995: 61), and her
first sexual awakenings "[score] her mind as a long drill scores the
crumbling sods of a brown, still, May" (71). On realising she is pregnant, she does not wake her husband "for this was her rig and furrow,
she had brought him the unsown field and the tending and reaping was
hers" (177), and later in her pregnancy "came that movement in her
body as she watched Ewan still – a mother with his child he was, the
corn his as this seed of his hers, burgeoning and ripening, growing to

harvest" (187). Chris's identification with the land stretches beyond the reproductive, however, and becomes implicated in her perception that "nothing endures but the land". Such an equation of the female body with the land may of course be used to help substantiate an extended "Chris Caledonia" reading, particularly since the parallel of Chris with the land lays emphasis on her qualities of fertility and endurance, both components of the nation-as-woman construction. The structure of *Sunset Song* also parallels her with the symbolic national landscape, marked by the landmark of the standing stones, the vantage point from which the story is narrated. Through her assimilation with the land she herself takes on this enduring quality. The implication is that the iconic female figure is outside history, a constant which serves as a backdrop to the action of male existence.

Despite this, as Brian Morton points out, Chris "is not an abstract and romantic personification of a nation like Yeats' Kathleen ni Houlihan" (Morton 1980: 202). The psychologically realistic characterisation of Chris herself makes any such identification problematic. There is an allegorical aspect to her representation but it does not fully correspond to the necessarily abstract and mythological woman-as-nation figures already considered. Chris resembles neither Britannia nor Cathleen ni Houlihan. On the contrary, reading Robert Colquhoun's "Chris Caledonia" statement in context suggests that she represents the national character rather than the nation itself. When Robert asks Chris if it feels "tremendous and terrible" to be pregnant, she answers only that "it made you feel sick, now and then" (139). It is this undemonstrative and reductive humour which earns her the title of "Chris Caledonia": she represents a typically Scottish character. As Thomas Crawford puts it:

If an observer says that a person is "Scotland herself", and if the remark applies to character, he can only mean that her personality reflects and embodies what the observer conceives to be the *national* character. (Crawford 1989: 122)

That is, rather than being an abstract and one-dimensional concept such as Britannia, Chris embodies a national typicality in a manner similar to John Bull. She proves the exception to Marina Warner's rule that the female allegorical figure is generic while the male is individual (Warner 1996: 12).

In his novels of the same period, Neil Gunn uses the female body and the landscape in a very similar way to Gibbon, although Gunn's

Scottish landscape is that of the Gaelic-speaking Highlands rather than
Gibbon's North-East. Gunn's women too are associated with the fertility and permanence of the land and function as a crucial backdrop to
community life. In *Butcher's Broom* (1934), a novel which was intended to "be about women" (Hart 1987: 92), the central character,
Dark Mairi of the Shores, is represented as having a deep identification with the land itself:

[…] the valley is shaped as the eyes of Dark Mairi see it. A smooth shape of slender
flanks and fluent spinal ridges, of swelling breasts and wandering arms, brown-
skinned except where the region of its fertility lies softly grey-green with grass […]
(Gunn 1934: 12)

Christopher Whyte identifies Mairi as "Gunn's embodiment of Gaelic
Scotland" (Whyte 1995a: 31). Certainly in her identification with the
land and her symbolic presence throughout the book she occupies a
very similar space to Gibbon's Chris Guthrie. Gunn's construction of
Gaelic Scotland depends very much upon a strict delineation of gender
roles, which he describes in pseudo-anthropological detail. His
achievement in representing a Scottish community and its mythology,
particularly in *The Silver Darlings*, has led to his being described as
the greatest novelist of the Scottish Renaissance. However, Whyte has
questioned the "eulogistic" consensus of Gunn criticism on the
grounds of Gunn's representation of Gaelic culture and of gender. He
argues that Gunn's essentialising of both gender roles and the Gaelic
community are linked, and that Gunn uses a specific construction of
gender to underpin the structure of his "traditional", "natural" Gaelic
community. Gunn's prescriptive gender ideology, and iconisation of
an essential femininity, represent, for Whyte, aspects of an ideology
close to contemporary European fascism (Whyte 1995c: 66).

    The association of the female with both the domestic and natural
creates the illusion of a "natural" domestic femininity which is associated with the preservation of tradition. In Yuval-Davis and Anthias's
terms, women participate centrally in the ideological reproduction of
the collectivity and transmit its culture (1989: 7). In Gunn's *Highland
River* (1937), the female figure is once again removed from the narrative of history and paralleled instead with the unchanging backdrop of
the landscape and the natural landmark. In the following extract,
Kenn's mother Ellen stands watching her husband and sons go to
church, while she stays at home to cook the Sunday dinner:

So quiet and contemplative and abiding she is, that from the shelter of her skirts one may brave God and all the unknown and terrifying things that go back beyond the hills to the ends of the earth and the beginnings of time [...] she becomes the rock that throws its shadow in a weary land [...]

So long has she been outside the mysteries and cults and secret associations man has made for his own pleasure and importance, that she is beyond the ethic of each age and every age, as life itself is, and continues as life continues, and endures as the hills endure. (Gunn [1937] 1991: 89–92)

The mother here acquires the status of a natural landmark and functions as a refuge and a sanctuary: she has an existence outside the temporal world inhabited by men. While Gunn never explicitly figures woman as nation he posits women as essential to, yet outside, the cohesion of the (male) community, elevating them to a mystical plane while at the same time effectively denying them any individual agency. Richard Price, in his largely appreciative study of Gunn, acknowledges that Gunn's "affectionate characterisation of women [...] always runs the risk of a dangerous if well-meaning sentimentalisation" (Price 1991: 114). The "archetypal" mother figure is removed from civil society and any political agency, remaining a symbolic figure who possesses "little personal individuality" (McCulloch 1987: 74) and becoming not an individual but an iconic female figure who "endures as the hills endure".

Catherine Kerrigan discusses the stereotype of the good wife and mother, "perpetuated in nineteenth and twentieth century novels by male authors", who is the centre of order in the family and in the community, and points out that it is this idealised image of domestic womanhood, representing "order, community, continuity, stability [and] security" which is transferred to the symbol of the nation as a woman (Kerrigan 1994b: 107). The limited domestic roles of Chris Guthrie or Ellen Sutherland are essential to the woman-as-nation narratives of their respective novels. The female, maternal body becomes conflated with the space of home and, in Alasdair Gray's words, with the landscape of home (Gray 1984: 167), and thus preserves that domestic space, as she preserves the identity of the nation. She must endure, like the land or the hills, so that the national identity she preserves will also endure. Roderick Watson identifies Gibbon's Chris Guthrie with "Alba as a place outside time in which ultimate truth can be found in the spirit of place and by (feminine) intuition, rather than through reason, intellect and masculine control" (Watson 1992: 259). The specifically feminine virtues associated with the "spirit of place" preserve the "true" national spirit and are located outside the sphere of civil society, removed from the male world of politics and religion.


## Women of Scotland: Willa Muir and Naomi Mitchison

The most high-profile female representative of the Scottish National Party in the late twentieth century was Winnie Ewing, SNP MP for Hamilton 1967–70, and for Moray and Nairn 1974–79, and, from 1975 onwards, member of the European Parliament, where she has been dubbed "Madame Ecosse". Less elegantly, on home soil, her nickname for many years was the "Home Rule Housewife" (Burness 1994: 138). This label simultaneously demeans her and makes her more human and accessible. At the same time it shows how persistent is the association of the female, the domestic, and the nation, and how difficult it can be for a woman, even for a politician at the end of the twentieth century, to escape from the prescribed roles available to her. In the period of the Scottish Renaissance, women wanting to engage with nationalist politics and culture had to engage with a gendered symbolic structure which functioned perfectly for the male nationalist writers who used it, but which made it very difficult for women to find a space in the political or literary nationalist world. Helen Cruick-shank, once asked if she was writing anything, told a publisher that she would write a book called *The Domestic History of the Scottish Renaissance* (Cruickshank 1962: 187). Whether or not there was an element of self-irony in this, her choice of title puts her in her place. Cruickshank was a poet, but not generally considered to be one of the first order, and lived a life of "selfless devotion to poetry and its prac-titioners", in particular to MacDiarmid himself (McMillan 1997: 435). As Christopher Whyte points out, "the history of the Scottish Renais-sance Movement was presented [...] with women as helpmates offering succour and support from the wings" (Whyte 1995a: 28). MacDiarmid himself identified Cruickshank, in this domestic and supportive role, along with his wife Valda Trevlyn, as a manifestation of "the Scottish muse" (MacDiarmid [1943] 1972: 400–1). The ease with which MacDiarmid was able to locate his female friends in this mythical role, alongside his favourite literary muses such as Audh or Brigit, demonstrates how the gendered model of the Scottish Renaissance was not simply textual but spilled out into the gender roles of the writers of the time. Domesticity is sublimated. Just as the domesticity of women such as Chris Guthrie or Ellen Sutherland in *Highland River* is connected to their symbolic status and their affinity with the land, women seem to be valuable not as literary producers but because, associated with the maternal and the domestic, they are able to preserve a pure national character and identity.

Willa Muir and Naomi Mitchison, women writers of the Scottish Literary Renaissance, faced problems when they tried to engage with the gendered version of nationalism that characterised the period. Both, in their different ways, try to appropriate the figure of the female nation for their own purposes, but neither fully engages with or manages to challenge the gender implications of Scotland represented as a woman. Willa Muir has a strangely contradictory attitude to the domestic feminine ideal. In *Mrs Grundy in Scotland* (1936) she traces the pernicious effects of the fear of social inferiority, personified by the figure of Mrs Grundy, in England and then in Scotland. Mrs Grundy is a symbol of conformity and respectability in the eyes of society, the next door neighbour who needs to be impressed with success and propriety. She is a personification of a social fear that affects both men and women, but she is personified as a woman, possibly because she is so closely identified with the home. The home, for Mrs Grundy, should be a reassuring place, which preserves traditional values and shelters the family from changes taking place in the world outside. We meet again the familiar figure of the mother who preserves traditions, and who with her body reproduces the space of the home. Willa Muir identifies how in this model,

The women envelopped their men. They were environments for their families. The men had no occasion to remember that women too might be individuals with a turn for adventurous enterprise. (Muir [1936] 1996a: 45–46)

Muir develops this idea of woman-as-environment versus woman-as-individual and argues that in the late nineteenth century women "began to assert themselves as individuals rather than environments" (47).

The notion of woman as environment seems not to be straightforward for Muir, however, for while she seems to reject the identification of women with landscape and home which recalls the female spirits of place in the fiction of Gibbon and Gunn, her attitude is more ambivalent in her essay "Woman in Scotland", also published in 1936. Here she argues for the involvement of women in national movements, and blames the exclusion of women from political life on the relegation of women to the domestic sphere. Nonetheless her analysis of the structures of male and female authority concludes that "his is the concentrated authority of an individual, hers is the more diffuse, pervasive, atmospheric authority of an environment" (Muir [1936] 1996b: 2). In this essay Muir uses the idea of woman as environment to argue that the political world should be able to incorporate the different female relationship to space and authority. She relates the notion of environment to a Marxist reading, seeing capitalism as an artificially created environment encroaching upon the mother's circle of environmental authority, and then compares the domestic maternal environment with that of the State in terms of money management and responsibility (3).

This ambivalence regarding woman-as-environment can also be found in *Mrs Grundy in Scotland*, as the book goes on to explore what kind of influence Mrs Grundy (or Mrs MacGrundy, as Muir christens her) might have had in Scotland. In Scotland, the negative effects of Mrs MacGrundy are much more associated with religion than in England, particularly with the sanctimonious aspects connected to the Presbyterian observance of the Sabbath. Muir concludes, however, that although Mrs Grundy did gain hold of the Scottish social consciousness, things happened rather differently than they did in England, largely because the Scottish woman had a much lesser tendency to think of herself as an environment: "None of your environmental nonsense in Scotland. Ilka herring had to hang by its ain tail" (49). Muir attributes this to the much more individualist tradition of the Church of Scotland, as a result of which, she argues, Lowland Scotland undervalued women (50). Her arguments are already a little contradictory, since, while she does not seem to approve of the equation of woman with environment, still she seems to say that it is precisely the association of women with environment and community that the Church of Scotland does not appreciate. The result of this is that, she says, "in Scotland... women had less support and showed more individual character than anywhere, I think in Europe" (50–51). Although Scottish women suffered from a lack of recognition and support, paradoxically this led to them being individuals rather than environments, which is positive in the long run, and leads to them being less identified with the home than English women.

Strangely, no sooner has she established Scottish women as less environmental than their English counterparts, than Muir merges her portrait of the strong and self-sufficient individual Scottish woman with the personification of the nation:

Ah, you will say, Scotland, that "puir auld mither!" Yes, but also "Caledonia, stern and wild." A mother with any strength of character is bound to become a formidable personality after a lifetime of coping with selfish children. There were the two types of Lowland Scotswomen; the puir auld mithers and the formidable, possible wild prototypes of Caledonia. (Muir 1996a: 51)

Muir invokes two different types of the Scotland-as-woman figure here: the suffering mother and the strong mother. The powerful personification of nation as mother continues, and Muir gives us both sides of the coin: the active and powerful nation who leads and nurtures her citizen-sons, and the feeble and victimised nation who needs to be defended and supported. What is most interesting is the way that Muir slips effortlessly from the personification of the nation to the discussion of "types" of Scotswomen. She performs a similar manoeuvre in "Women in Scotland", where she argues that women should become more involved in political life, something which would involve a "right balance between environment and individual" (Muir 1996b: 4). She continues, "Scotland as a nation has been for so long a 'puir auld mither' that Scottish mothers are likely to have a fellow-feeling for her" (4). Muir's juxtaposition, in both these texts, of the metaphor of motherland with actual mothers, citizens of the nation, has a strange effect. She appropriates and challenges the woman-as-nation figure, and yet at the same time reinforces the ideology that supports the figure.

This double signification of the figure of the mother is somewhat vertiginous. The mother-nation metaphor, as traditionally used, excludes women from the subject position of citizen, because the female is subsumed in the abstract figure of the nation as mother to male citizens. The metaphor, although unacceptable from a feminist point of view, *works* when constructed in this way. The male nationalist sons of the mother nation are comforted by her and defend her. There is no space for actual mothers in the metaphor. When Muir juxtaposes the Mother Scotland figure with real, individual mothers, the dissonance between the two levels creates a sense of awkwardness.

On the other hand, however, Muir reminds us that the female figure cannot be separated from the flesh and blood existence of actual women. She cannot, it seems, evoke the female personification of nation without the figures of actual women appearing alongside her. Her allusion to Scott's "Caledonia, stern and wild" immediately leads her to discuss the formidable women who have haunted Scottish imagination and literature from the ballads to the novels of Scott himself (Muir 1996a: 51). Both the positive and the negative aspects of the figure of Scotland-as-mother lead her to make generalisations about the character of Scottish Lowland women rather than about Scotland itself. Rather than being another example of Warner's female container in whose skin all the citizens may live – "they stand for us regardless of sex, yet we cannot identify with them as characters" (Warner 1996: 12) – Muir's Caledonia represents Scottish women themselves. This recalls Thomas Crawford's assessment that Gibbon's "Chris Caledonia" referred more to the national character than to the mythical figurehead of nation (Crawford 1989: 122). Willa Muir dedicated *Mrs Grundy in Scotland* to the memory of Lewis Grassic Gibbon, and her appropriation of the figure of Caledonia, like his, may be an attempt to subvert the tradition of the empty figurehead of nation. There are still problems with Muir's use of the allegory: Scottish women must be mothers in her model, it seems, and the paralleling of Scotland and woman as victims in the role of the "puir auld mither" reproduces one of the most problematic aspects of the woman-as-nation figure. Nonetheless, she provides a way out of some of the more limiting constructions of women in the literature of the Scottish Renaissance, and finds a way to put real women back on the literary map.

Naomi Mitchison also merges the voice of Mother Scotland with the voice of a real woman in her long poem "The Cleansing of the Knife 1941–47", though, as with Muir, her move is not entirely successful. In the poem Mitchison herself takes on the voice of "Alba our mother", and addresses a nationalist son. With her move to Scotland in the late 1930s, Mitchison began a process which her biographer describes as "writing herself into Scotland" (Calder 1997: 149), and this required her to evaluate what constituted a "Scottish tradition" both in literature and in historical scholarship. Mitchison's position not only as an aristocratic outsider but as a woman writing into a masculine construction of Scotland clearly influences her reactions to and negotiations with such a tradition. In "The Cleansing of the Knife", she declares, manifesto-like, "I am a woman of Scotland" (Mitchison 1978: 39), thus asserting her own position within Scotland and within the poem. The interaction of the subject positions of woman and Scot create a powerful dynamic within her writing, because her insistence on her existence as a "woman of Scotland" stands in direct contrast to MacDiarmid's effective polarisation of the terms "woman" and "Scot" in *A Drunk Man Looks at the Thistle*. By bringing the two terms together, Mitchison defines a place in society for herself and defines herself in terms of the two aspects of her existence she feels to be most important – as she puts it in her diary in 1942, "feminism and Scotland, the things I *feel* about" (Mitchison 1985: 217).

In her poetry and fiction, Mitchison explores ways in which Scotland and its history have been constructed, and at the same time she is concerned with personally contributing to the construction of a positive and practical vision for Scotland's future. In "The Cleansing of the Knife" she identifies the problems facing Scotland and ends by proposing a solution. Within this basic structure she uses images and vocabulary similar to MacDiarmid and other writers of the Scottish Literary Renaissance. In her attempt to fit into the Scottish tradition she situates herself in a Renaissance context whose parameters had been fixed some ten years earlier. However, she struggles to accommodate herself within this context partly because of her paradoxical political and class position and partly because of her gender. The sequence of poems is thus torn between her desire to integrate herself and her text into the Scottish Renaissance and her desire to assert her own feminist and socialist beliefs within this Scottish context. The narrative structure of the poem is based on a relationship between the narrative voice of the poem (who I will call "Mitchison" for ease of reference, since biographical details make it almost impossible to separate narrator and author) and a man called "Donnachadh Bàn", to whom much of the poem is addressed. It seems that Donnachadh Bàn was based on an estate worker at Carradale, and the socially unequal relationship between laird and estate worker is worked into the poem (Calder 1997: 167). The pseudonym Donnachadh Bàn also ties the poem to a Scottish literary heritage as it refers to Duncan Bàn MacIntyre, the eighteenth-century Gaelic poet. Within the structure of the poem, the social difference between them is translated into the voice of a mother speaking to her son, but the mythologised mother, the voice of mother Scotland. Thus Mitchison casts herself as "the voice of Scotland, / Alba our mother" while Donnachadh Bàn becomes the archetypal "Highlander, son of Alba" (Mitchison 1978: 40). The relationship of "Alba our mother" to her son solves, at least temporarily, Mitchison's two problems of identification. Her social position is removed from its political implications and instead gains a mythical status. To speak with the natural authority of "Alba our mother" overrides the ironies of her actual situation as an aristocratic incomer who is imposing her ideas for improvement upon her local community; it also gives her an acceptable position which had already established within the Scottish Renaissance context from which she can find a voice to speak.

Although she succeeds in finding a voice for herself within "The Cleansing of the Knife" she still leaves many problematic gender issues unresolved. The problems that surround the sequence of poems and the sense of an unsatisfactory conclusion all serve to highlight the difficulties facing a woman trying to write specifically about Scotland in this period. The only voice which seems to be available to Mitchison is of the mother-nation herself, rather than the position of nationalist-poet. Speaking "with the voice of Scotland, / Alba our mother" could be seen as a positive strategy by which the hitherto passive personification of Scotland is given a live female voice. However, Alba quickly assumes the position of innocent victim who has suffered many wounds and disappointments over the centuries, particularly in part x of the poem, where every verse concludes with variations on the line "Alba our mother, what have we done to thee?" (Mitchison 1978: 64). Although Mitchison writes herself into her own history, the figure of "Alba our mother" is still being used for emotive purposes. The mother-figure of Scotland is someone who suffers the actions of other people.

A similar construction of the suffering female body as Scotland occurs in Mitchison's 1947 novel *The Bull Calves*, which in other ways offers a very positive construction of Scotland. Beth Dickson describes it as

[...] a late example of the novel of the Scottish Literary Renaissance with its emphasis on rebuilding Scotland agriculturally, politically and culturally to make it a confident member of the international community. (Dickson 1987b: 38)

In this historical novel, based on her own family history and set in the uncertain political climate immediately following the Jacobite uprising of 1745–46, Mitchison insists that every account of history, and indeed of nationhood, must necessarily be a construction (Stirling 1999). The past in *The Bull Calves* is composed of stories, narrated by various characters in the novel. Of all the various stories, Kirstie's is by far the largest sustained narrative in the book. Although there are also stories told by and to men in the novel, it is Kirstie's story which is privileged, and it is Kirstie who functions as a linchpin between all the different strands of narrative, between her husband and her family, and between Highlands and Lowlands. Both through her own personal experience and through the political lives of her Haldane brothers she is connected to many of the major events in eighteenth-century Scottish (and in some cases, extra-Scottish) history. With the character of Kirstie Haldane, Mitchison moves from the use of woman as a symbol of nation to the representation of women as characters in history. The emphasis on the oral transmission of history and the domestic setting of the Haldane family home give a new perspective to a period which is more often overshadowed by the very male fields of politics and war.

Kirstie's stories to Catherine, occupying the largest single element of the novel, suggest a matrilineal inheritance of history. But Kirstie is more than a teller of tales: she is a "woman of Scotland" who has participated in the history of her nation and who is therefore able to narrate her own role in this history. The stories she tells include the domestic experience of history within the narratives of war and politics of the period. Kirstie recounts the after-effects once the Jacobite army had burnt a series of villages near Stirling, and the help that the family was able to give the villagers (Mitchison 1947: 67–68); she tells of her own efforts to help the miners in Ayr after an accident in the pit (98–99). She also explains why she sheltered a hunted kinswoman with Jacobite connections in the aftermath of the 1745 uprising (384–85). And her main narrative, again running counter to conventional history, is of her own experiences as a member of a witches' coven. Such narratives have the effect of humanising the processes of history, and it is this sense of humanity and practicality which governs the stories of history that Kirstie tells to Catherine.

As Kirstie narrates history to Catherine, and the men discuss agriculture, the narrative voice tells us "the minds of the two women

were again on people and not on things" (77). Kirstie's narrative to
Catherine begins with her half-joking statement that men are nothing
but bairns, whereas women "are for ever needing to take thought for
the morrow, aye and the morrow's morn. We canna afford to be gen-
erous and daft the way the men are, more's the pity" (38). Mitchison
consistently emphasises women's different vision of history and
allows women the possibility of effecting change. She plays with the
ways in which women's different relationship to nation and different
attitude to history might be represented, and, like Willa Muir, compares the management skills of a housewife with those necessary to
run a government:

If a' the governing of the world were left to the women of it, they would never do the
daft-like things the men do, throwing away their own lives, aye and others'. The
world could surely be managed the way a household is, cannily. (38)

This fantasy is one way of rewriting women's political disen-
franchisement and may be read as a vision of a potential matriarchal
society, suggested also by Mitchison's emphasis on the female transmission of history and matrilineal line of descent (Plain 1996: 156–
57).

Kirstie's central position makes her truly a "woman of Scotland",
the position Mitchison claims for herself in "The Cleansing of the
Knife", but she is also able to take on the mantle of "Alba our
mother", and like the figure of Alba, her body too becomes a metaphor for Scotland's suffering. We learn in the stories which are told
throughout *The Bull Calves* that Kirstie has suffered, but in the present
day of the novel her maternal body is a symbol of hope and of
regeneration. Like Chris Caledonia in Gibbon's trilogy, Kirstie is only
twice explicitly compared with Scotland, and in each of these
instances the comparison rests on Kirstie's status as victim and the
political position of Scotland. William recalls his first meeting with
the newly widowed Kirstie after his return from America. Her mental
confusion at this time and her belief in witchcraft are represented
physically by her almost wanton appearance as she opens the door of
her house in a state of undress. William, being a gentleman, does not
take advantage of the situation, but rather thinks, "And maybe, lassie,
you were like poor Scotland herself, and one more betrayal would
have spoilt you clean" (Mitchison 1947: 170). Kirstie's vulnerable
female body, sexualised and left open to attack from outside, clearly

conforms to the flip side of the chaste and impregnable body of the defended nation. Scotland is not defended, and is open to betrayal from both without and within. William's rhetoric of betrayal also locates Kirstie, and Scotland, in the position of innocent victim. Like Alba our mother, she is *done to*; she suffers the actions of others.

The other explicit parallel drawn between Kirstie and Scotland comes earlier in the book. Kirstie's unhappy marriage to her first husband, the minister Andrew Shaw of Bargarran, moves Lachlan Macintosh of Kyllachy to remark, "Ah, poor lassie, poor wee lassie [...] She is fast in her trap as poor Scotland herself, and as fully eager to bide there" (106). Again the parallel is based on Kirstie's position of victim, but Kyllachy's comparison goes in a slightly different direction from that of William and allows for the interpretation that both Kirstie and Scotland are to some extent responsible for their respective predicaments. Mitchison thus uses Kirstie's story to suggest an allegory of Scotland as a woman both trapped and betrayed. But unlike the figure of Alba our mother in "The Cleansing of the Knife", the metaphor of Kirstie as Scotland is never allowed to dominate the narrative or to remain the governing image of woman in the text.

Both Mitchison's and Muir's use of nation-as-woman imagery differs from the male construction in that the mystical aspect of female existence is removed, and the emphasis is on women as individuals within the political economy and within the narrative. However, both women's feminist re-appropriation of the mother Scotland figure includes a comparison of Scotland and women on the grounds of their shared victimhood. In both cases, when the abstract allegorical figure of nation clashes with the narrative of an individual character, the result is Muir's "puir auld mither". The narrative of Scotland as a suffering woman provides a compelling plot structure, but once we start to examine the implications of the woman-as-victim allegory, it soon becomes clear that it is problematic, not only regarding the representation of women, but also regarding the representation of Scotland.

# Chapter Three

## The Female Nation as Victim

The discovery of America by Amerigo Vespucci is allegorised in a drawing by Jan van der Straet of around 1575 (see Montrose 1993: 179–80; de Certeau 1988: xxv–xxvi). In an erotic interpretation of the explorer's first encounter with America, the new world is feminised as a Native American woman, naked, reclining on a hammock. Vespucci stands before her stiffly, while she, although slightly startled by his appearance, assumes an inviting posture, rising from her hammock to greet him. Her hammock is strung between two trees which frame the scene of the as yet undiscovered land behind her: thus her body is the gate to the new world. To proceed, the explorer will have to pass through her body. Here the feminised land invites domination. In a fantasy of female submission, the female nation is imagined as voluntarily and lasciviously offering herself, and this opens the door to a long history of America mythologised as "virgin land" waiting to be discovered and penetrated by male science (see Kolodny 1975). In an image which may be read similarly, the figure of Britannia which forms the frontispiece to Michael Drayton's elaborately illustrated *Poly-Olbion* (1612–22) sits in the centre of a triumphal arch, clothed in a cloak representing the British landscape, surrounded by fruit representing fertility. Laurent Berec argues that by situating Britannia in the centre of the arch on the title-page, the designer of *Poly-Olbion* constructs her body as the portal through which one has to pass to enter English territory (Berec 2000).

In images such as these, the female body does not simply function as the figurehead of the nation, or as the vessel which contains the national essence. As the nation is mapped onto the symbolic female body, the contours of her body reproduce the boundaries of the nation, and the threat of invasion and breach of the national boundaries becomes metaphorically represented by the threat of penetration of the body. In wartime various forms of patriotic imagery become widely used, and the image of "the nation as a loved woman in danger", evoked by Yuval-Davis and Anthias (1989: 9–10), gains a particular resonance. The female body is vulnerable to attack and must be protected. The "reinforced" female body described by Marina Warner

(1996: 258) strengthens the contours of the body to allow it to carry the weight of its allegorical contents, but also, particularly in the case of Britannia, signifies her chastity and inviolability, representing both the nation's defences against external invaders and the preservation of national purity: a closed system of reproduction. Although Britannia's martial imagery gives an impression of power, her elaborate defences at the same time suggest the possibility of invasion. The valorisation of female virginity is directly connected to the fear of invasion of national territory. The chaste body of the nation is a guarantee of national security. If the "wholeness" of the national body is penetrated, the nation loses integrity and is open to exploration and/or domination by external forces. This metaphor persists in the rhetoric of modern war reporting, where the word "rape" is used in titles such as *The Rape of Kuwait*, a popular book after the Gulf War (Sasson 1991). The archaic definition of the word "rape" – "The act of taking a thing by force; *esp.* violent seizure of property, etc." (OED) – is invested with contemporary moral horror at rape as a sexual crime. Such titles re-emphasise the symbolism of the idea of the homeland as a female body which must be defended against violation (Parker et al. 1992: 6). But on a real, physical level this type of symbolism becomes action in, for example, the atrocities committed during the war in former Yugoslavia. An EU investigation team estimated that 20,000 Muslim women were raped in Bosnia between April 1992 and January 1993 (Enloe 1993: 240). If women are seen as signifiers of the boundaries of ethnic groups/nations then the rape of women is the ultimate invasion of territory.

The representation of the woman-as-nation figure as a sexual being, therefore, generally has a negative connotation. Female chastity is valorised, and to be defended at all costs, and the logical opposite of chastity is violation. The female figurehead may be objectified, raped or prostituted, in order to signify the degradation of the nation. The threat to the national body may not simply be that of foreign invasion. There is also the danger of corruption from within, in the form of political mismanagement inappropriate to the dignity of the chaste mother-nation. By the middle of the eighteenth century, Britannia had been represented as "innocent virtue outraged […] variously dismembered, buggered, ridden and even flogged naked with 'a Scottish Thistle'" (Dresser 1989: 34). The female body lends itself to such allegorical representation, and the construction of the chaste mother figurehead perhaps even invites it, because the violation of the female body gains significance with the breaching of the defences of that chastity. The very fact that the earliest known image of the Britannia figure symbolises the Roman conquest of Britain by showing the emperor Claudius overpowering a supine and sexualised Britannia, suggests that the allegory of violation is written into the nation-as-woman figure from the beginning. (Dresser 1989: 26; Warner 1996: 45–46).

Florence Stratton defines this type of allegory as "woman [serving] as an index of the state of the nation". Writing about African literature by male writers, Stratton identifies two strands of what she calls "the Mother Africa trope". In the first, woman is seen as the container of an unchanging African essence. In the second, in order to indicate the political domination of Africa, the Mother Africa figure is represented in servitude, abandoned, raped or in prostitution (Stratton 1994: 41–44). This "index of the state of the nation" use of the female body develops from the mother-as-nation allegory, because in order for the metaphor of exploitation to work, there must exist an idealised and non-abused female body. If the female body functions as an index for the state of the nation, her degradation shows how far she has fallen from the status proper to the vessel of the primordial national essence. The construction of woman as victim is one of the most problematic aspects of the woman-as-nation allegory, and yet one of the most fundamental. The idea that women are always victims or potential victims underwrites almost every representation of nation as woman.

We have already seen a tendency towards this "index of the state of the nation" metaphor, in Willa Muir's assessment of Scotland as a "puir auld mither" (Muir 1936: 4), and in the repeated lament of Naomi Mitchison's "The Cleansing of the Knife": "Alba our mother, what have we done to thee?" (Mitchison 1978: 39). Interestingly, for these two female writers of the Scottish Renaissance, to describe Scotland as a mother equalled describing her as a victim. The resonance of the metaphor is difficult to escape, and indeed, the figure of the disappointed mother forms the basis of one of the earliest instances of Scotland as woman that I can determine, Dame Scotia of Robert Wedderburn's *Complaynt of Scotland* (c.1550). The "affligit lady dame scotia", as she is described, appears to the poet in a dream and he recounts the way in which she reprimands her three sons, the

Three Estates, for the divisions that threaten to destroy Scotland (Wedderburn [c.1550] 1979). Much of the attraction of the Scotland-as-woman figure is in this parallel of Scotland and woman in the position of victim.

## Politics and Pornography: Alasdair Gray's *1982, Janine*

Alasdair Gray's *1982, Janine* (1984) stands out as a prime example of "woman-as-state-of-the-nation" symbolism in modern Scottish literature, although Gray treats the trope very self-consciously and plays with the mixture of attraction and revulsion written into it. *1982, Janine* takes place in the mind of Jock McLeish, as he passes a solitary drunken night in a hotel room somewhere in Scotland. Jock's thoughts wander from sexual fantasy, to memories of his youth and first love, to political commentary on the state of Scotland. The sexual fantasies are sado-masochistic, based on scenarios of bondage and rape, and Jock moves through a series of similarly structured fantasies involving different woman – Janine, Superb, Big Momma – who find themselves lured into situations where they lose control and are subjected to a variety of ingenious sexual tortures. The metaphor of woman as nation here depends on the exploitation of women, and it is made fairly clear that the sexual exploitation in Jock's fantasies may be read in political terms. When Jock claims that "Scotland has been fucked and I am one of the fuckers who fucked her", he explicitly states that the word "fuck" is used "in the vulgar sense of *misused to give satisfaction or advantage to another*" (Gray 1984: 136).

Gray tells us in *1982 Janine*'s "Epilogue for the discerning critic" that "the matter of Scotland refracted through alcoholic reverie is from MacDiarmid's *A Drunk Man Looks at the Thistle*" (Gray 1984: 343). But the gender politics of Gray's novel may also be traced back to *A Drunk Man*. As with MacDiarmid's women in *A Drunk Man Looks at the Thistle*, a clear line can be drawn between Gray's construction of the wholesome, maternal woman associated with the land and with home, and his less tangible "fantasy" women who expand the possibilities of the metaphor. But while MacDiarmid's ethereal woman possesses a hint of illicit sexuality, Gray's fantasy women are specifically located in the context of sexual fantasy. The pornographic fantasies are however complemented and paralleled by

Jock's attitude to his first girlfriend Denny in the "realist" section of the novel.

In Jock's nostalgic memories of his youth, Denny is described in terms of landscape and home. Jock's natural and uncomplicated relation to Denny is connected to a "natural" relation to nation, and a nation which is defined, unchangeably, by the contours of its landscape. At one point Jock realises that the map of Scotland resembles "a fat messy woman with a surprisingly slender waist" (Gray 1984: 281), and this identification is extended to the geography of Scotland in its entirety. Denny is a "real" woman. She exists as a memory as opposed to a fantasy. Janine and the other fantasy women, however, are invented, and their imagined bodies function as metaphors for more abstract and political processes. There are two different uses of the female body here, and two different ways of representing a nation. The nation is seen either as an immemorial and eternal space to which we have a natural connection, or as constructed by arbitrary political processes. In simplistic terms, the body of Denny represents the romantic idea of the nation, while the body of Janine represents the politicised body of the state. The pornographic sexual fantasies of bondage and rape function as an allegory for colonial exploitation and specifically for the perverted and unnatural political processes acting upon the stateless nation of Scotland. However, the very fact that in *Janine* the fantasies are *imagined* suggests that the political exploitation is also constructed and has the potential to be changed.

Critical reactions to the pornographic aspect of *Janine* range from downright condemnation of its exploitation of women to a tendency, among more liberal critics, to explain, if not excuse, the pornography. The objectification of the female body, the various sadomasochistic acts and, perhaps most problematically, the fact that the fantasy women eventually seem to enjoy their experiences of kidnap and rape, have all excited a great deal of critical comment. Stephen J. Boyd criticises Gray's pornography as a "black art" (Boyd 1991), questioning the justification of printing material which might encourage emulation of Jock's fantasies. Eilidh Whiteford comments that even if Gray's use of the word "pornography" alludes to the Victorian values the novel seeks to debunk and Victorian inhibitions it seeks to dispel, the issue at stake remains whether or not he is justified in his use of explicit imagery (Whiteford 1994: 80). Critics who deplore the pornography often display a certain prurience, speculating about

Gray's own consumption of pornography ("even if it is all a parody, one must have a good working knowledge of whatever it is one wishes to parody") and discussing whether the fantasies are actually Gray's own: "But Alasdair Gray *publishes* his fantasies" (Boyd 1991: 112; 118). The vision this perpetuates, of Gray as a dirty old man thrusting his fantasies upon the world, ignores the political metaphor contained within the pornography. Despite the validity of questions regarding the use and representation of women's bodies, such knee-jerk reactions ignore the subtleties of Gray's project.

Other critics act as apologists for Gray's use of pornography by explaining its moral function. Christopher Gittings asserts that the pornography in *Janine* is "not employed to titillate the male reader" but to "sicken and repulse the reader" (Gittings 1995: 34). Douglas Gifford describes how the fantasies are

[...] in fact a brilliant way of demonstrating how Jock's sickness is the world's.[...] [The fantasies] are finally meant to disgust, to shame us; we have all helped spawn these stereotypes of male domination [...] (Gifford 1987: 114)

The emphasis on shame, disgust and repulsion distracts attention from the fact that these fantasies may indeed titillate the reader and may in fact be designed to do so. But, as Christopher Whyte mischievously comments, "what (heterosexual) critic wants to risk putting his (or her) own fantasies on the line?" (Whyte 1995b: xvi–xvii). Of course the readership of *Janine* cannot be assumed to be unanimous either in opinion or in sexual fantasy. However, for Gray's political allegory to be fully understood it seems necessary to emphasise that while disgust, shame and repulsion are elements of the recipe, they should be acknowledged as accompanying a certain sexual pleasure. The pleasure that is derived from pornographic fantasies which include "women dehumanised as sexual objects, things or commodities, enjoying pain or humiliation or rape" (*Pornography and Sexual Violence* 1988: 2) is perhaps not divisible from shame. However, it is pleasure nonetheless. But if critics and readers refuse to admit that there may be any pleasure at all to be gained from the fantasies – and political correctness may make them disinclined to do so – they are ignoring a vital aspect of the book. Jock's perverse pleasure in the political and social trap in which he is caught is mirrored in his fantasies.

There is no coherence to the pornographic narratives, which are fractured by the intrusion of the memories which Jock is trying to suppress, and by his lapses into political diatribe. In David Lodge's phrase, "the *coitus interruptus* of Gray's narrative technique" assures that the reader, along with Jock, is never likely to achieve any satis-faction as a result of the fantasies (Lodge 1984: 45). Jock's "recipe for pornography" (Gray 1984: 29) at the beginning of Chapter Two high-lights this process, as he compares his technique for delaying orgasm to the method of a historian describing the build up to war. As Jock switches between his various fantasy women, building each up to a state of excitement and then abandoning them to begin another story, so the historian switches between countries:

[...] showing depression and dread growing within each for domestic reasons, but dis-tracted by challenges and threats from abroad [...] and then the tanks start rolling through the streets with evacuations, concentration camps, explosions, firestorms, frantic last-minute propaganda and the awful togetherness of total calamity before the last, huge, final, bang. *That* is how a big piece of pornography should go. (Gray 1984: 29)

This "recipe for pornography", situating Jock's fantasies in the context of western political history, suggests that the very structures and plots of pornography are already inscribed within our society, and indeed a female friend of Jock's points out to him the "convincing political structure" of his fantasies (67). But the most telling political message of the fantasies concerns the responsibility of the individual, and the abdication of responsibility which is sanctioned by the fantasies them-selves. Jock's fantasies are set not in Scotland but in America because, says Jock, "Seen from Selkirk America is a land of endless porno-graphic possibility" (17). But by situating his fantasies in America, Jock is able to disguise the fact that his fantasies have such a bearing on his own political situation. And this distance which Jock has imposed between his real life and his fantasy life is most significant in the reversal he describes in this passage, which functions as a far more telling "recipe" for the pornography employed in the novel:

I had started telling myself stories about a very free attractive greedy woman who, confident in her powers, begins an exciting adventure and finds she is not free at all but completely at the disposal of others. As I aged that story grew very elaborate. The woman is corrupted into enjoying her bondage and trapping others into it. I did not notice that this was the story of my own life. I avoided doing so by insisting on the *femaleness* of the main character. The parts of the story which came to excite me most were not the physical humiliations but the moment when the trap starts closing and the victim feels the torture of being in two minds: wanting to believe, struggling to

believe, that what is happening cannot be happening, can only happen to someone
else. And I was right to be excited by that moment because it is the moment when,
with courage, we change things. (Gray 1984: 193–94)

This masterful reversal, where Jock suddenly claims to have been
identifying with the women in his fantasies rather than with the sadistic male villain, could be seen (cynically) as a neat way to sidestep the
worst accusations regarding the exploitation of the image of the
female body. But it is more than that. If Jock has been identifying with
Janine and Superb, that is, if the fantasies are masochistic rather than
sadistic, this changes their whole dynamic. If we return to the Janine
and Superb fantasies, we realise that the women function as the
narrative consciousness of the stories, and it is their excitement (a
crucial aspect of the fantasy) that Jock experiences. In chapter one,
"Janine's feeling that she is watching *herself* increases, filling her with
a numb, dreamy excitement. The excitement has a spice of fear in it
but not much" (24). In chapter two, "[Superb's] skin tingles and a
dreamlike feeling comes to her, for the woman is holding up a white
denim, no white suede button-through skirt…" (40). Janine's "numb,
dreamy excitement" and Superb's tingling "dreamlike feeling" represent the prelude to sexual arousal. Thus the women, although represented as sexual objects, are the narrative subjects of their respective
stories; the fantasy narrative is refracted through the consciousness of
Janine or Superb. The fantasy women (and Jock) are excited by the
moment at which they lose control: "the moment when the trap starts
closing". The fantasies are all structured around the idea of the trap,
and the "depression and dread" of Jock's previously quoted "recipe
for pornography" is experienced by his heroines in the moment,
narrated by Jock, that they realise the trap is closing and they have
become victims.

The sections of the novel identified as "Jock's autobiography"
explain the various "traps" he has been caught in during the course of
his life, and the present day narrating instance of the novel sees him as
a lonely alcoholic, in a job he hates, in a hotel room in a politically
and financially impoverished country. He articulates the traps, both
personal and political, in which he finds himself, by displacing his
experiences onto a female character who exists in a context in which
such traps are not only the norm but the required formula. Jock's
excitement at the closing of the trap, and the fact that his fantasy
women experience this as sexual excitement, is linked to the problem-

atic question of the myth of women being turned on by rape. Jock's fantasies depend upon this, which could be considered their most offensive and potentially dangerous aspect. It is claimed that exposure to pornographic material, *particularly* that containing the idea that women could be turned on by rape, leads to acceptance of these types of myth on the part of the subjects (Donnerstein 1988: 15). Although such an argument on the part of the anti-pornography lobby may well have some validity, Sara Diamond, writing in *Women Against Censorship*, theorises the phenomenon of women fantasising about rape in a more exploratory and enabling manner:

If we fantasise a partner taking complete control of a sexual encounter, then we are absolved from responsibility for our abandoned behavior. In this way we can mentally break sexual taboos that still remain in place in practice. (Diamond 1985: 51)

It is this notion of being "absolved from responsibility" which is crucial to the fantasies in *Janine*. The pleasure and excitement experienced by Jock at the moment when the trap closes emphasise the perverse sense of pleasure he takes in his own powerlessness. Once the trap is closed there is nothing the "victim" (whether Jock or Janine) is able to do to change things so (s)he is able to abdicate all responsibility for the situation. Politically, this abdication of responsibility absolves Jock, or the people of Scotland, from admitting participation in the processes which have "fucked" the nation. The fantasies allow Jock the dual status of both admitting and denying responsibility. Jock retains authorial control of the fantasies, a control denied to his heroines. Thus it is he who creates the trap, but by identifying with the position of the victim he avoids responsibility for it.

To consider yourself a victim is very attractive because it removes any responsibility – both responsibility for the position in which you find yourself and any responsibility for extricating yourself. To claim that the fantasies are meant to inspire disgust and revulsion in the reader misses the point that what the fantasies deal in most of all is the self-indulgent attraction of the victim position. And this has an obvious application to the situation of Scotland. In her guide to Canadian literature, *Survival*, Margaret Atwood works out a list of "basic victim positions", which, she explains, "are like the basic positions in ballet or the scales on the piano: they are primary, though all kinds of song-and-dance variations on them are possible", and may be applied to victimised countries, minority groups or individuals. She

makes very visible the leap from the individual victim to the national
victim: "Let us suppose, for the sake of argument, that Canada as a
whole is a victim ... If Canada is a collective victim, it should pay
some attention to the Basic Victim Positions" (Atwood 1972: 35 36).
These "Victim Positions" range from "Position One: To deny the fact
that you are a victim" to "Position Four: To be a creative non-victim."
Most interesting in relation to *Janine* is Position Two:

> To acknowledge the fact that you are a victim, but to explain this as an act of Fate, the
> Will of God, the dictates of Biology [...], the necessity decreed by History, or Eco-
> nomics, or the Unconscious, or any other large general powerful idea". (37)

Atwood's concern is with Canada, but much of what she says might
be applied to Scotland. The political aim of *1982, Janine* is not simply
to illustrate a version of Atwood's victim position two, but to illustrate
the political futility of such a position and the possibility of accepting
responsibility and moving on.

In *Janine*, Jock has informed us that the true moment of excitement in the fantasies is "the moment when the trap starts closing and
the victim feels the torture of being in two minds ...the moment when,
with courage, we change things" (Gray 1984: 194). The political
"trap" is illustrated throughout Jock's fantasies by the bondage clothes
in which the women are dressed – one staple ingredient of the fantasies is that near the beginning the heroine is told what to wear by her
agent/lover/procurer (Gray 1984: 13; 31; 323). Under the marginal
heading "Clothes that are bondage", Jock's description of Janine's
attire gives way to an autobiographical passage relating the way in
which his mother's choice of clothes for him dictated to a certain
extent the pattern of his educational and social life (18). Much later,
Jock acknowledges the ultimate benefit of this to him: "My mother, by
a skilful use of clothing and emotional blackmail, trapped me into
doing my homework so as to free me from the long town and she
succeeded" (215). Just as the dungarees worn by the "rough boys", the
colliers' sons, in Jock's childhood make an appearance in the fantasies
on the person of Superb, a symbol of illicit dirtiness and roughness
(75), so the notion of clothes as a trap, but a trap which is ultimately
beneficial, informs the central motif of the fantasies. The sexy paraphernalia in which Jock attires each of his heroines is the visual manifestation of the trap in which they find themselves. Jock's description
of his childhood experience of clothing again implies a certain

security in the removal of responsibility. The idea of security, particularly given Jock's job with "National Security Ltd", is closely linked to the idea of a *trap*. Both the sado-masochistic and slavery connotations of bondage become transformed into this sense of security.

Janine's final appearance in the novel is an escape from the security/trap of the known and the scripted, a rewriting of that moment "when the trap starts closing" (194). Instead of following the instructions of her anonymous employer, she changes things, thinking "Hell, no! Surprise them. Shock them. Show them more than they ever expected to see", and embarks on a striptease:

Standing easily astride she strips off her shirt and drops it, strips off her skirt and drops it, kicks off her shoes and stands naked but for her net stockings. I need the stockings. A wholly naked woman is too dazzling so she stands naked but for fishnet stockings, hands on hips and feeling an excited melting warmth between her thighs. She is ready for anything. (341)

Janine's striptease enacts the process of transition from bondage to freedom. The implication of the erotic moment "when the trap starts to close" becomes transformed from the potential for victimisation into the potential for change. Jock's refusal to imagine a naked woman because she will be "too dazzling" may mean that his ideal landscape will be forever fettered by the perversions and injustices of political processes which abuse, distort and diminish. But there is always the potential to remove the bondage to reveal the naked and true self. This self may be Jock, or may be his true vision of Scotland. As God admonishes Jock: "come out of the sexy accessories Jock McLeish! We know you're hiding in there" (331).

## "We was robbed": Scotland as victim

*1982, Janine* is a creative deconstruction of the woman-as-index-of-the-state-of-the-nation symbolism. Gray makes visible the processes whereby the female body is allegorised for political purposes and he also makes visible a tendency towards willed victimisation in Scottish culture. As the poet, playwright and short-story writer Janet Paisley puts it, "Witness [Scotland's] favourite sayings a) it wiznae me b) we wuz robbed c) a big boy did it an run awa" (Paisley 1999: 75). In a short article which appeared in a special edition of the *Edinburgh Review* marking the advent of a devolved Scottish Parliament, Paisley mocks Scotland's "limiting notion of victimhood" by using the metaphor of the female nation as victim. She begins her short piece by using the nation-as-woman allegory, but undermines it and ridicules it in a such a way as to deliberately expose the ideologies of victimhood latent in any use of the allegory, and suggests that it is precisely in defeating such assumptions that Scottish literature may progress healthily towards the future. She begins:

It's the story, you see. There was this nubile young virgin forced into marriage by the big bad landowner next door […]. And while her feisty heroic kin made a great hullaballoo, an uncharacteristic slowness affected their wits and the dirty deed was over and done before they could unsheathe a claymore. (Paisley 1999: 74)

*The* story: the definite article deftly indicates the prevalence of this myth of the Scottish situation. Scotland, in this narrative, is defined as the innocent victim, forced, unconsenting, into Union. The emotive rape metaphor comes into play, and the image of the nubile young virgin emphasises Scotland's blamelessness. This very symbolism was used in Mel Gibson's *Braveheart* (1995): in the first episode of Wallace's adult life he witnesses the abduction of a white-faced Scottish bride by a tyrannical English landowner claiming his *prima nocte* rights. Central to such a metaphor, however, is Scotland's powerlessness and inability to escape from the role of victim. The raped virgin is the epitome of victimhood, and this is the key to the nation-as-woman metaphor. But Paisley continues:

Maybe it's this story. There was this knocked about a bit teenage lass who longed for tattoos, bit of body piercing, some easy glamour and whose youthful form had long been coveted by the baldy middle aged git with the bulging wallet next door. So what's a girl to do? And anyway, she wised up soon as she realised when you trade your liberty for brass, brassed off at being another chattel is all you get. So she got herself a divorce, quick as a flash, so she did. Oh, aye?
    Actually not. She wimped, and wheedled and whined and, rather than own up to covetousness or risk the poverty of single life, invented story one. (Paisley 1999: 74–75)

Here Paisley uses the nation-as-woman allegory in order to undermine another long-lived myth of Scottish history. The historical circum-stances of the Treaty of Union between Scotland and England in 1707 are unique. There is no doubt that England put a great deal of economic, political and indeed military pressure on Scotland to ensure the union of the two countries ("blackmail" and "bribery" are the more emotive terms often used), but the Treaty of Union remains a Treaty between two independent countries and the responsibility lies with the Scottish nobles who signed it. "Sic a parcel o' rogues in a nation", as Robert Burns remarked, but even in Burns's version, the rogues are undeniably Scottish. As Paisley emphasises with the "bulging wallet" of the man next door, Scotland did indeed have much to gain economically from Union with England, partly because of the failure of Scotland's only colonial enterprise, an attempt to establish a colony on the isthmus of Darien (Panama), which had come to grief in 1698–99 and resulted in major losses for Scottish investors. There is irony in Scotland's lost statehood resting on its own attempt at colonisation, and this further complicates any attempt at a post-colonial reading of Scotland. By putting this twist on the story, Paisley strips the Scotland-as-woman metaphor of its key ingredients, Scotland's blamelessness and victimhood. In story two Scotland is culpable not only of covetousness but of a refusal to acknowledge responsibility. This dismantles the ideology of self-perpetuating victimhood that surrounds the allegory.

Like Gray, Paisley uses the woman-nation-victim allegory in order to undermine it. She ridicules it and in doing so dismantles its implicit ideology of victimhood, making it clear that Scotland as woman is not only a negative image for women, but that its implications for our perception of Scotland are also negative. Any nation-as-woman allegory which depends, even obliquely, upon the equation of woman with potential victim is necessarily reductive and perpetuates a sexist ideology in which women are always the passive recipients of someone else's actions. But the allegory not only simplifies and limits lived female experience, it also simplifies and limits Scottish history, and results in a dead-end position where Scottish nationalists abdicate responsibility and point the finger of blame at England. Identification with the position of victim is not a productive strategy for nationalist thought either, and yet Scotland as victim is a myth that continues to permeate Scottish society. What is rather disturbing is that the tradition of comparing women with Scotland on the grounds of shared victimisation can be found in critical writing, and indeed in feminist critical writing by critics who are seeking to challenge the gender stereotypes they find in Scottish literature and culture.


## Multiple Oppressions

In Scotland, many women seeking to reconcile their feminist and nationalist beliefs have experienced a frustration not unlike that experienced by black feminists in America. Using a piece of domestic imagery, Joy Hendry in 1987 described the situation facing Scottish women as the "double knot on the peeny". Hendry explicitly situates Scotland within the colonial context by describing it as an "oppressed colony of England," and uses the colonial exploitation of Scotland to explain the internal exploitation of Scottish women:

Being a woman is difficult enough. But being a Scottish woman is more difficult still because of Scotland's position as an oppressed colony of England, and a nation with severe psychological hang-ups. There is this popular myth that the Scottish male is more domineering, his attitudes to women more "primitive" than other men. Certainly, we have the same problems as women everywhere, but perhaps in more extreme form. (Hendry 1987: 36)

Marilyn Reizbaum uses the same critical approach when she suggests that:

The need to define nationalism in patriarchal terms in countries that have struggled against a colonising "father" is perhaps a response to the historical figuration of cultural "inferiority" in stereotypes of the feminine. (Reizbaum 1992: 172)

Both articles postulate that the patriarchal nature of Scottish culture is a reaction to stereotypes of cultural inferiority imposed upon Scottish culture. Hendry identifies the loss of Scottish nationhood as "an experience something like castration" and concludes that this experience, together with poverty, the injustices of Scottish history and the erosion of Scottish culture, has "brutalised the Scottish male" (Hendry 1987: 36). This metaphor works on two levels because, while the individual Scottish male is brutalised, it is evidently the Scottish nation which has suffered castration through the loss of its organ of political power. This image of the Scottish nation as emasculated, and therefore tending towards the feminine, is an interesting corollary to the "state of the nation" metaphor. The titles of each of these articles focus on the idea of "doubleness" as a crucial factor in women's engagement with their national identity, whether as citizens, readers, or writers. This doubleness is expressed as a double oppression: Scottish women occupy a position of inadequacy not only because they are Scottish but because they are also women.

Much feminist theory states that all forms of oppression are linked in society and are supported by similar institutional structures. Black American feminists, by conceptualising feminism as "a struggle against sexist oppression", allow recognition of the fact that men may be equally oppressed, on grounds of race or class. Thus feminism, as a struggle against oppression, must necessarily incorporate a struggle against all forms of oppression: race, class, and national (hooks 1984: 35; see also Walker 1984; Lorde 1984). Black women may suffer from the sexism of black men, but they can equally recognise that this chauvinism comes from the male's sense of himself as powerless in relation to ruling male groups, rather than expressing a privileged social status (hooks 1984: 18). However, the idealistic aims of such theorising are not so easy to achieve in practice. The discourse of nationalism is able to subsume the oppression of women into its master narrative and represent it as one of the many injustices which will be overturned when the principal aims of the movement are achieved. Thus in many nationalist struggles we witness the recurring myth which implies or states explicitly that gender oppression follows directly from national oppression. If there is an identifiable oppressor, that oppressor must be responsible for all forms of oppression, including sexist oppression, and if there exists a golden age myth, it is a construction of an age in which no form of oppression existed. In Irish Republican ideology, therefore, the contemporary subjugation of Irish women is a direct result of the conquest of Gaelic Ireland and the destruction of its ancient egalitarian traditions, while Welsh nationalist ideology emphasises the better treatment of women under the medieval laws of Hywel Da (Ward 1983: 254–55; Davies 1996: 166). The incorporation of one struggle against oppression within another is merely nominal and one of these struggles therefore becomes devalued and ignored. In such a pattern the feminist struggle is invariably subordinated to the nationalist. So Virginia Woolf was able to write in 1938 that "as a woman I need no country", and much more recently, in a Scottish context, Liz Lochhead claimed that she did not really consider herself to be a nationalist or even primarily a Scottish poet, since, as she put it, "until recently I've felt that my country was woman" (Woolf 1938: 197; Nicholson 1992: 223).

Marilyn Reizbaum's study of the "double cross" suffered by Irish and Scottish women is a specifically "canonical double cross". Countries like Scotland and Ireland, struggling against exclusion from and marginalisation within the Anglo-American canon, notably exclude women from their own canons (Reizbaum 1992: 166). There is a strong parallel between the feminist challenge to the male canon and the challenge presented by "Scotland, Ireland, and other countries like them" to the mainstream Anglo-American establishment. Reizbaum goes on to suggest that writers who are able to work towards a "dynamic relation of movements, in this instance, nationalism and feminism" provide a more "revolutionary" solution to both problems (168). The parallel which she highlights between women and colonised countries lends itself to further development, but while the initial motivation for comparison of the two seems legitimate enough, extended development of the parallel often risks reproducing conservative ideologies.

## Gender theory and the nation

This more theoretical approach to the intersection of nation and gender demonstrates that the two struggles in fact contain the same structure, and that lessons might be learned from applying feminist theory to national or post-colonial struggles, or conversely, applying post-colonial theory to the situation of women. This approach avoids the somewhat defeatist attitude of the first school and does provide many valuable insights. Despite its very modern and theory-driven credentials, however, such an approach contains highly conservative elements, not least its tendency to reproduce the equation of woman with nation, along with all the dangers and contradictions inherent in the allegory.

Both post-colonial and feminist criticism have made explicit comparisons between the exploitation of women and of colonised peoples. Each field draws on the discourses and terminologies of the other to express the politics of oppression:

Women in many societies have been relegated to the position of "other", marginalised and, in a metaphorical sense, "colonised" [...] They share with colonised races and peoples an intimate experience of the politics of oppression and repression. (Ashcroft et al. 1989: 174–75)

The parallels drawn between the "othering" of women and the colonised are based on the premise that all forms of oppression function in similar ways. They also provide useful insights into ways of ordering resistance to the power structures in action in each instance. Similarities in the very language used to characterise the "other" in both female and racial oppression also encourage such parallels:

[...] in the language of colonialism, non-Europeans occupy the same symbolic space as women. Both are seen as part of nature, not culture, and with the same ambivalence: either they are ripe for government, passive, child-like, unsophisticated, needing leadership and guidance, described always in terms of lack – no initiative, no intellectual powers, no perseverance; or, on the other hand, they are outside society, dangerous, treacherous, emotional, inconstant, wild, threatening, fickle, sexually aberrant, irrational, near animal, lascivious, disruptive, evil, unpredictable. (Carr 1985: 50)

The very fact that oppressed nations suffer from many of the same stereotypes and power structures as women do has led many critics to attempt a reconciliation of the two fields of study. Instead of an emphasis on the subordination of one form of oppression, or the "multiple" or "double" nature of the female position within the nation, we witness an interchange of critical and theoretical methodology between the two fields, on the level of theory rather than practice.

This type of cross-disciplinary exchange between feminist and post-colonial theory has a slightly longer history than the fairly recent advent of studies incorporating feminism and nationalism. Nationalist theory in general paid very little attention to gender until the topic began to be tackled from a feminist angle in the late 1980s, with studies such as Kumari Jayawardena's *Feminism and Nationalism in the Third World* (1986) and Yuval-Davis and Anthias's *Woman-Nation-State* (1989). Studies such as Benedict Anderson's *Imagined Communities* (1983) and Ernest Gellner's *Nations and Nationalism* (1983) espoused a modern and constructionist view of nation which, rather than analysing the citizen's relationship to a pre-existing state, began to analyse the process whereby the idea of the nation is created by a communal consensus (see also Smith 1971 and 1987; Hobsbawm

1990). While this new method of theorising the nation represents a
liberating and exciting approach to the subject, and one which had a
great influence on literary critics, all these books may be and have
been criticised for their "androcentric perspective" (Davies 1996:
170):

[…] as insightful as Ben Anderson's and other landmark books of this era were in
charting new ways to think about the creation of nationalist ideas, they left nationalists – and pre-nationalists and anti-nationalists – ungendered. Our understanding of
nationalism suffered. (Enloe 1993: 231)

The perceived masculinity of the processes of the nation state is reproduced in the theory of the construction of nation, which is concerned with a male subject, or at best, an ungendered, universal subject who is assumed to be male.

In *Imagined Communities* Benedict Anderson introduces the
question of gender by remarking that "everyone should have a nationality as he/she has a gender" (Anderson 1983: 14). He does not, however, question this statement, and this almost throwaway use of the
word gender has been picked up by Eve Kosofsky Sedgwick:

To suggest that everyone might "have" a nationality as everyone "has" a gender pre-
supposes, what may well be true, and may well always have been true, that everyone
does "have" a gender. But it needn't presuppose that everyone "has" a gender in the
same way, or that "having" a gender is the same kind of act, process, or possession for
every person or for every gender. (Sedgwick 1994: 148–49)

Anderson was writing in 1983, Sedgwick in 1994, and the gap
between them illustrates the considerable change in both the visibility
of gender theory and the theoretical direction of nationalist theory in
the intervening ten years. Sedgwick is able to use gender theory to
destabilise a fixed notion of national identity, in the same way as
feminist theory is now able to access the discourse of post-colonial
theory to describe women as "colonised".

Various critics have transferred this interchange of methodologies into the Scottish context, despite the fact that defining Scotland as
postcolonial is in itself rather problematic. While an analysis of the
cultural relationship between Scotland and England could be said to
match the colonial model, an extended post-colonial analysis of the
Scottish situation seems impossible. Nevertheless, Scottish literary
critics have been flirting with post-colonial criticism for some time,

some going all the way and some maintaining their critical distance (see Schoene 1995; Murray and Riach eds 1995). Perhaps the inclusion of Scotland in a post-colonial context is intended to give Scottish studies a legitimacy outwith the immediate (parochial) context of Scotland. The application of feminist theory to Scotland, following the postcolonial model, is intended to open up new avenues for discussion and also perhaps to find some way of reconciling the feminist and the nationalist in Scottish studies, given the sense of double oppression expressed by critics such as Joy Hendry, Carol Anderson and Glenda Norquay (Anderson and Norquay 1984).

In the introduction to *Gendering the Nation* (1995), Christopher Whyte attempts to illustrate the relevance of gender theory for nationalist theory by taking a passage on gender theory from Judith Butler's *Gender Trouble* (1990) and substituting "Scottish" for "feminist" throughout (Whyte reproduces the deleted words in square brackets immediately after the words which have replaced them):

> The postulation of the "before" within Scottish [feminist] theory becomes politically problematic when it constrains the future to materialise an idealised notion of the past or when it supports, even inadvertently, the reification of a pre-Union [pre-cultural] sphere of the authentic Scottish [feminine]. This recourse to an original or genuine Scottishness [femininity] is a nostalgic and parochial idea that refuses the contemporary demand to formulate an account of nationality [gender] as a complex cultural construction. This ideal tends not only to serve culturally conservative aims, but to constitute an exclusionary practice within Scottish theory [feminism], precipitating precisely the kind of fragmentation that the ideal purports to overcome. (Whyte 1995b: xii; see Butler 1990: 36)

Whyte quotes this passage to illustrate "how much those working in the related fields of gender, sexual orientation and nationalities have to learn from each other" (Whyte 1995b: xiii). The passage is adroitly chosen, as the situation described by Butler is almost uncannily appropriate to certain "golden age" constructions of Scottishness. Whyte's emendation of this passage thus creates the powerful illusion of a link between gender and nation. However the serendipity of this similarity does not mean that gender theory can be applied in its entirety to theories of national identity, within Scotland or without. While nationality is without question a "complex cultural construction", it is not constructed in the same way as gender. Although Whyte states that he is simply suggesting ways in which the two fields may "learn from each other", what he actually does is to substitute one term for another throughout the passage. This suggests that the structures and methodologies of one field may be applied wholesale to another, which is a highly problematic move.

The most extended use of this cross-disciplinary approach in the Scottish context is found in Susanne Hagemann's article "A Feminist Interpretation of Scottish Identity" (1994). Hagemann, indeed, explicitly claims that she is "retaining the structures and arguments of [...] feminism, and applying them to the literature of region and nation in their entirety". She does not, in fact, go on to fulfil this intention entirely, acknowledging later in the article that "in some fields, e.g. sexuality on the one hand and political independence on the other, significant correspondences do not come readily to mind" (Hagemann 1994: 79; 89). But she takes two feminist approaches to literature, "feminist critique" and "gynocriticism" – that is, images of women in literature by men, and criticism of literature written by women – and transfers the methodology of each approach to a regional/national approach to Scotland. Her use of feminist critique falls at the first hurdle because, unable to find a sufficient number of examples of descriptions of Scotland from an English point of view, she is forced to doctor her data and deals instead with texts containing descriptions of the Highlands from a Scottish Lowland perspective (Hagemann 1994: 81). Her appropriation of "gynocriticism" is more persuasive and follows a similar pattern to the method used by Whyte. She takes Elaine Showalter's periodisation of women's writing into three broad periods, "feminine", "feminist" and "female", and finds corresponding phases in the history of Scottish literature. Showalter's periodisation is as follows:

First there is a prolonged phase of *imitation* of the prevailing modes of the dominant tradition, and *internalisation* of its standards of art and its views on social roles. Second there is a phase of *protest* against these standards and values, and *advocacy* of minority rights and values, including a demand for autonomy. Finally there is a phase of *self-discovery* a turning inward freed from some of the dependency of opposition, a search for identity. (Showalter 1977: 13; cited in Hagemann 1994: 86)

Hagemann identifies a "regional" or "provincial" phase, marked by "conscious Anglicisation"; a "nationalist" phase in the twentieth-century Renaissance; and a "national" phase, which is "self-consciously Scottish to such a degree that it feels no need to define itself in opposition to England" (Hagemann 1994: 88). Hagemann admits that she is functioning on a different timescale to Showalter, and finds no feminist parallel for Scotland's pre-Union stage of "non-peripheral autonomy" (87).

It is in the section on feminist critique, however, that this theorising runs aground. Hagemann parallels patriarchal discourse with Anglocentric discourse and discusses the representation of both Scotland and woman as "other". Such an approach depends upon transforming "images of woman" criticism into "images of Scotland", and comes dangerously close to reproducing the metaphor of Scotland as a woman. The theory indeed requires us to compare Scotland to a woman. Hagemann uses Malcolm Chapman's list of stereotypes of the Celt in order to justify her parallel of women and Scotland. Both women and Celts have been constructed as more emotional than intellectual, as intuitive rather than rational, as closer to nature than culture and concerned more with family than society (Chapman 1978: 106). Chapman's list of binary oppositions does prove that women and Celts are subject to similar mechanisms of stereotyping. However the fact that Celts have been stereotyped *as feminine* should not be used to validate further critical interpretation along the same lines. Hagemann's analysis verges on the ridiculous when she extends her categories of centre and periphery to suggest that we may consider the Highlands by connecting them to lesbianism: "if lesbians can arguably be considered the most radical woman-identified women, the Highlands, more precisely various aspects of Gaelic culture, are very often seen as the epitome of Scottishness" (Hagemann 1994: 85).

Applying feminist theory to the study of the nation appears inevitably to reproduce the metaphorical equation of nation equals women. Such criticism offers very little that is valuable or positive to a female writer or reader attempting to come to terms with the contradictions inherent in her position. What it suggests is a return to the type of nation-as-woman metaphor in which woman acts as the "index of the state of the nation". The attempt to escape from oppression through a revisualisation of the problem creates its own problems, and ultimately succeeds only in closing down possibilities for development rather than opening them up. Although the motivation behind such theorising is progressive and intended to break down categorisations, it risks coming full circle and returning to the allegory of woman as nation. Criticism that parallels the position of women in society with the position of Scotland perpetuates an ideology in which

both women and Scotland are constructed as victims, and thus reproduces the ideologies implicit in the fictional constructions of nation as
woman throughout the twentieth century.

# Chapter Four

## The Monstrous Muse

In *1982, Janine*, Alasdair Gray made visible an important subtext to the nation-as-woman figure: that the allegory virtually requires her to be a victim. The fantasies of *1982, Janine* demonstrated how the external appearance of the symbolic woman, as in a pornographic fantasy, is a male construction, and how a male script determines the role she has to play. Gray is evidently fascinated by the use of a woman to represent nation or state, and enjoys going beneath the surface of the symbolic female body to find out how the metaphor works. In *Poor Things* (1992), Gray pursues the idea of the male construction of the female figure by giving us a Scotland-as-woman figure – "Bella Caledonia" (Gray 1992a: 45) – who is literally constructed by the Frankenstein-like Godwin Baxter. This continued exploration beneath the skin of the Scotland-as-woman figure uses the Frankenstein story to show how she is necessarily distorted or deformed in some way.

As we saw in the examples from the Scottish Renaissance, there is always something wrong with the Scotland-as-woman figure. Either the weight of allegory proves too heavy for the shoulders of the fictional character, as in the case of Gibbon's "Chris Caledonia", or the female figure is split in two by the contradictory roles she has to fulfil, as we saw in the work of Hugh MacDiarmid. Gray represents this distortion or gap literally. He presents us with the image of a beautiful woman who represents the nation and who holds the country together. Traditionally, her external integrity and beauty form the shell that contains the essence of the nation and the political structures of the state. However, when internal divisions become too great to be contained within her shell, it begins to crack or become deformed in some way, revealing its internal workings. Gray's Frankenstein-like narrative makes visible the distortions to which the nation-as-woman figure – but particularly the Scotland-as-woman figure – is subject. The Scotland-as-woman figure is pulled in different directions by the clash of national and political boundaries, and this is reinforced by a critical tradition that sees Scotland and Scottish culture as essentially divided.

## Body as state: Alasdair Gray's *Poor Things*

The portrait of "Bella Caledonia" in *Poor Things* (Gray 1992a: 45)
suggests that Gray wants us to read the character Bella Baxter in the
tradition of nation-as-woman iconography. Bella's "tall, beautiful and
full-bodied" exterior (29) would seem to qualify her for the statuesque
role of national figurehead, and she is situated, with a plaid over one
shoulder and thistles on her hat, in a recognisably Scottish landscape
(we see the Forth Railway Bridge over her right shoulder). But the
Frankenstein-esque plot of *Poor Things* ensures that Bella can never
be an uncomplicated representation of nation – if such a thing can ever
exist. In her body she combines both the external appearance of the
romantic woman-as-nation figure and the idea of the body politic, and
the disjunction between these further distorts the image of woman as
nation which at first sight she appears to encapsulate.

*Poor Things* is a parody of a Victorian novel, and like Shelley's
*Frankenstein* itself, it is constructed from three overlapping narratives.
The volume is edited and annotated by a fictional editor called
Alasdair Gray. The central narrative is the story of the literal physical
creation of a woman called Bella Baxter, by the surgeon Godwin
Baxter, from the body of a woman and the brain of a child, and is
written by her husband Archibald McCandless, M.D. This is followed
by a letter by the woman herself, styling herself Victoria McCandless,
refuting the entire story of her *Frankenstein*-like construction and
giving a perfectly realistic account of her arrival in the house of
Godwin Baxter in Glasgow. The dual narratives of *Poor Things* allow
at least two readings of the novel: the fantastic narrative, based on
McCandless's account of the Frankensteinian construction of Bella;
and the realist narrative, based on Victoria's more straightforward
account of her life. Both readings, however, prompt questions regarding women being constructed to correspond to male fantasies, as
*either* Bella is constructed by Godwin Baxter, *or* the entire tale is a
fabrication of Archie McCandless. The theme of the construction of
the self is emphasised by Gray's chapter titles: "Making Me" (9),
which describes the childhood and upbringing of Archibald McCandless; "Making Godwin Baxter" (12), which suggests the literal construction of Baxter; "Making a Maniac" (75) which is a letter from
Duncan Wedderburn describing his elopement with Bella and charting
his descent into insanity; and "Making a Conscience" (103), a letter

from Bella herself in which we witness her growing sense of social awareness. Gray emphasises that we are all constructed both in the sense of what we become and in the sense of how we are perceived by other people. In *Poor Things*, both these types of construction focus primarily on Bella.

Gray dangles the "Bella Caledonia" tag tantalisingly in front of the reader but leaves it very much up to us whether or not to engage with its implications. There are many other paths of enquiry to pursue in *Poor Things*, and because of its multi-layered narratives it is able to support – and indeed encourage – a number of different readings and interpretations. "Bella Caledonia" may be an incitement to locate Bella in the tradition of women as nation, but if we were to dismiss the nickname as mere hyperbole, as indeed Victoria's letter to posterity insists that we must, then it would be possible to read the entire novel without imposing a nation-as-woman reading upon it (Gray 1992a: 251).

The suggestion of a nationalist subtext is reinforced, however, by the design on the cover (under the dustjacket) of the hardback edition, which has a pattern of Saltires and elongated Scottish thistles with the legend "Work as if you live in the early days of a better nation". This slogan recurs in a number of Gray's books. It is first found in *Unlikely Stories, Mostly* (1983) under the dustjacket of the first edition and on the first page of the paperback, accompanying a picture of a topless woman who appears to be a mermaid with a tartan tail, perhaps the first manifestation of Scotland as a woman in Gray's work. Just as *Poor Things* offers us the choice between a "blurb for a popular paperback" and a "blurb for a high-class hardback", the hardback lets us choose whether to leave the dustjacket on. But once we have looked beneath the dustjacket this gives much greater weight to a reading in which Bella is Bella Caledonia, and her Frankenstein construction may be read as a political metaphor. If Bella is Caledonia, her ambiguous status implies that Scotland is certainly a construct, and probably a monster.

In *Why Scots Should Rule Scotland* (1992), Gray situates Scotland in the tradition of representing the nation by a female figurehead:

Since the 18th century sculptors and political cartoonists have often represented nations as single people, usually robust and beautiful women with names like La France, Italia, Germania. If Scotland were so depicted the head would have to be shown attached to the body by a longer neck than the poor lady's height; moreover the head would also be attached by a neck of normal length to a different and much stronger body. No wonder many Scottish limbs and organs are underfed, numb and disconnected from each other. Too many of them cannot act without orders from a remote head which is distinctly absent-minded toward them because it must first direct a far more urgent set of limbs and organs. (Gray 1992b: 58–59)

In this passage we can see the process whereby Gray arrives at his monstrous version of Scotland. He associates Scotland with other, less problematic nation-states, whose essence is contained within the vessels of their institutional female figureheads. He also shifts the ground of the metaphor. The "robust and beautiful women" he describes are generally figureheads, representing the outward face of the nation. The stretched and deformed Scotland-as-woman he describes represents the political situation of Scotland. Gray is tapping the tradition of using the body as a metaphor for the political processes of the state, which has a long history but is quite distinct from the use of the female form as the incarnation of the nation.

The idea that we can explain the workings of the state by analogy with the human body goes back at least to Plato's *Republic*. The concept is perhaps most famously represented in the frontispiece to Thomas Hobbes's *Leviathan* (1651), which depicts the giant figure of a king rising out of the landscape, wielding a sword and a sceptre. The body of this figure is made up of many smaller bodies: the bodies of the citizens. The body of the state in this metaphor is composed of people who all perform distinct functions yet all depend upon each other, as the various organs of the human body working together form a "unity of diversity". The Leviathan image depends on an organic conception of the state: each individual citizen performs the work of an organ of the body. According to Hobbes's introduction, the king is the head of this body, sovereignty is the soul which gives life and motion to the body, the magistrates and officers are joints, reward and punishment are nerves, wealth and riches are strength, counsellors are memory, equity and laws reason and will. Therefore, concord is health, sedition is sickness and civil war is death (Hobbes [1651] 1996: 9). From this it follows that disorder in the state can be represented as a sickness. The idea of "unity of diversity" is dependent upon each member of the state performing his or her function and all parts working together. If each part does not know its place and do its job then the notion of a deformed body (of state) develops (Barkan 1975: 61; 79). If a nation's political system is personified in terms of human anatomy, a nation whose political system is malfunctioning is then personified as a monster.

Gray's interest in the Leviathan image can be seen in his use of a version of it as the frontispiece to the fourth book of *Lanark* (1980), and in his comment on Hobbes's introduction in his *Book of Prefaces*:

> [Hobbes] does not believe he is using a poetic metaphor when he describes men and their nations as different sizes of mechanical doll; he thinks he is being modern and scientific. [...] [T]he long sentences of the Introduction keep stimulating us with spiky little aphorisms in the Baconian style, but jauntier and more persuasive than Bacon, because for all the scientific pretension of this metaphor he is using the same sort of wit Donne uses when he describes the body of his mistress as an ocean full of undiscovered lands. (Gray 2000: 279)

Here Gray makes explicit the overlap between the two connected metaphors of the state functioning as an organic body, and land or the nation represented as a female body. If the "streight Hellespont between / The *Sestos* and *Abydos* of her breasts" of John Donne's "Elegy: Love's Progress'" (Donne 1971: 123, ll.60–61) is thus superimposed onto Hobbes's "artificial man", the generally male (or asexual) body politic begins to take on some of the characteristics of the romanticised female embodiment of nation. At the same time the closed and statuesque female figurehead becomes prone to the deformities that may afflict the body of state.

The traditional woman-as-nation figure exists independently of the citizens of the nation (Warner 1996: 12). And when she exists as a mother, or as a lover, she is a figure with which citizens (usually male citizens) can interact. She may function as a container, but then, as Gray puts it in *Why Scots Should Rule Scotland 1997*, "a great mixture of people has poured into this irregularly shaped national container, a mixture to which people still add themselves" (Gray 1997: 4). In this model the nation is a pre-existing container which may be filled by the people who inhabit it. The nation and the citizens are independent bodies, whereas in the Hobbesian body-as-state model the citizens form an essential part of the body of the nation, and without the bodies of the citizens there would be no nation. In his *Anatomy of Britain*, Anthony Sampson describes his interviewees as "the arms and legs and the main blood stream" of the nation (Sampson 1962: 87). Gray conflates the much more visceral imagery upon which the body-as-state model depends with the chaste, whole and aesthetically attractive body-shell of the female nation. And therefore, when Gray pursues this conflation of ideas, Scotland becomes represented as a deformed female body. In fact, Gray suggests that she must be deformed in two ways at the same time: both a "longer neck than the poor lady's height" and the monstrous existence of "a different and much stronger body". While this imagery is used to make a point about the effect on Scotland of being part of the United Kingdom, and to suggest that monstrous political processes are at work, it also rather suggests that Scotland is *necessarily* deformed in some way. According to Gray's rather brutal logic, if Scotland is to be represented as a woman, she cannot be anything but deformed, intrinsically divided between Scottishness and Britishness.

Such a deformed body, however, would be virtually impossible to write into a work of fiction, but in the figure of Bella Baxter (Bella Caledonia) Gray is able to demonstrate the metaphorical distance between her head and her body without resorting to physical monstrosity. It is Bella's internal construction, the placing of her infant brain within her adult body, which allows her to function as the incarnation of the monstrous and deformed body of state. Her monstrosity is emphasised through the many intertextual links between *Poor Things* and Mary Shelley's *Frankenstein*, and further through the use of many details from Mary Shelley's biography. Aspects of Mary Shelley's Monster and Mary Shelley herself meet in Bella. The very name of the creator in *Poor Things*, Godwin Bysshe Baxter, not only has the convenient abbreviation "God", but is also stitched together from parts of William Godwin, her father, Percy Bysshe Shelley, her husband, and William Baxter (less obviously perhaps), the father of the family in Dundee with whom Mary Shelley was sent to stay at the age of fifteen. Echoes of Mary Shelley's life can be seen in Bella's unorthodox upbringing, the absence of any mother-figure – Mary Shelley's mother, Mary Wollstonecraft (1759–97), author of *Vindication of the Rights of Women* (1792), died eleven days after Mary's birth, of puerperal fever – and her pseudo-deification of the father-figure in her life. And the circumstances in which Bella's body comes into Baxter's hands, the recovery of the body of a pregnant woman from the Clyde, would appear to be derived from the suicide of Shelley's first wife, Harriet, who drowned herself in the Serpentine in December 1816, reportedly while pregnant (Small 1972: 178).

Bella's external beauty, her "tall, beautiful and full-bodied" appearance (Gray 1992a: 29), which qualifies her so perfectly to be one of the "robust and beautiful women" that Gray describes in the *Why Scots Should Rule Scotland* passage, may be related to the traditionally accepted photogenic and attractive appearance of Scotland which masks the monstrous political reality. This external physical attractiveness makes her different from Frankenstein's monster, whose monstrous appearance is transferred, in *Poor Things*, onto Baxter. There is a strong hint in the novel that Baxter may himself have been created by his father using the same techniques which he used to reanimate Bella. In her letter disputing the fantastic narrative Victoria McCandless writes: "[Archie] wrote a book suggesting that [...] God had always been as Archie knew him, because Sir Colin had manufactured God by the Frankenstein method" (Gray 1992a: 274). Baxter is a fusion of Frankenstein and the monster: he fulfils the promise inherent in Frankenstein's dying words to Walton: "another may succeed" (Shelley [1818] 1996: 187) and at the same time takes on the Monster's monstrous appearance. Yet the status and definition of monstrosity are problematised in *Poor Things*. Bella is never described as a "monster"; the word is used in relation to Baxter only four times in the course of the novel, and only *after* he has created Bella. As soon as McCandless understands that Baxter has created Bella using the brain of a child, Baxter carries him upstairs and McCandless "thought [he] was in the grip of a monster" (Gray 1992a: 31). He then goes on to challenge Baxter: "How dare you talk of your lovely niece in that monstrous way" (36), which sets up the opposition between Bella's exterior "loveliness" and Baxter's monstrous description of her creation. McCandless later, during a conversation about Bella's creation, says that he felt "more of a monster than [Baxter] was" (40), and the description of Bella opposite the Bella Caledonia portrait is contrasted with a description of Baxter:

[...] if she seemed a glorious dream Baxter loomed beside her like a nightmare. When apart from Baxter my memory always reduced his monstrous bulk and shaggy boyish head to something more probable [...] (44–47)

The words "dwarfish" and "ogreish" are used in the first physical description of Baxter (12), and his physical abnormalities are hinted at, but it is only when he is described in relation to Bella, or when his creation of Bella is evoked, that the loaded word "monster" is used. In

*Poor Things* the word seems to be reserved less for the creature than for the creator who flouts the laws of nature.

Gray goes one step further than Shelley in creating a female monster. It is the fear of female sexuality and consequent reproduction which prevents Frankenstein from creating a mate for his Monster:

> [...] she, who in all probability was to become a thinking and reasoning animal, might refuse to comply with a compact made before her creation. [...] one of the first results of those sympathies for which the daemon thirsted would be children, and a race of devils will be propagated upon the earth, who might make the very existence of the species of man a condition precarious and full of terror. (Shelley [1818] 1996: 114)

In *Frankenstein* it is the *potential* of the female monster both to reproduce and to reason for herself which is a threat. Frankenstein's fears about creating a female monster centre on his lack of knowledge of the mysterious and dangerous "disposition" of the female. The male monster is created: Frankenstein does not consider the consequences of his actions, and then the monster goes on to act on his own account. The female monster, however, exists only as a potential space which Frankenstein and the reader fill with predictions and preconceptions, just as Bella's body exists for the men in the novel as a space to be filled with preconceptions of virtue or vice, and the infancy of her brain within her adult body makes it a space to be filled with the thoughts of others. This is another way in which Bella is "monstrous". Unlike Frankenstein's monster, the stitching together of her various parts is not externally visible. However, in the process of "Making Bella Baxter" (Gray 1992a: 32) her knowledge of the world, and of its literature, is stitched together from a variety of different sources. She begins as an empty shell, rather like the statuesque woman-as-nation figure, and she acquires her contents gradually. As she tells McCandless:

> the few wee memories in this hollow Bell tinkle clink clank clatter rattle clang gong ring dong ding sound resound resonate detonate vibrate reverberate echo re-echo around this poor empty skull in words words words words wordswordswordswordswordswordswordswordswordswords that try to make much of little but cannot. I need more past. (61)

The stitching together of words in her brain is illustrated by her letters back to Baxter and McCandless in the "Making a Conscience" section (103–89). The curiously consonantal mode of her earlier writing is compared by McCandless to "the ancient Hebrews and Babylonians" (56); later her writing takes on the language and form of Shakespeare (101; 105 ff). During her world tour she absorbs, repeats and questions the opinions of the people she meets. Her developing conscience is made up of a patchwork of encounters just as the text is, as Victoria puts it in her letter denying the central narrative, a mixture of "all that was morbid in that most morbid of centuries, the nineteenth" (272). She goes on to specify that McCandless

has made a sufficiently strange story stranger still by stirring into it episodes and phrases to be found in Hogg's Suicide's Grave with additional ghouleries from the works of Mary Shelley and Edgar Allan Poe. What morbid Victorian fantasy has he NOT filched from? I find traces of The Coming Race, Dr. Jekyll and Mr. Hyde, Dracula, Trilby, Rider Haggard's She, The Case-Book of Sherlock Holmes and, alas, Alice Through the Looking-Glass; a gloomier book than the sunlit Alice in Wonderland. He has even plagiarised work by two very dear friends: G.B. Shaw's Pygmalion and the scientific romances of Herbert George Wells. (Gray 1992a: 272–73)

This passage has the same function as Gray's "Index of Plagiarisms" in *Lanark* (Gray 1981: 485–99), or the "Epilogue for the discerning critic" in *1982, Janine*. (Gray 1984: 343). Gray admits his so-called "plagiarisms" and by doing so, turns them into intertextuality. At the same time, by revealing his method of stitching together a patchwork text from a variety of sources, he makes the text more complex. Bella is explicitly paralleled with the composite text of *Poor Things*, not only in the insistence on the literary development of her writing, but also visually, as on the spine of the dustjacket of *Poor Things* we see the head of a woman, dissected to make the brain visible, held between the pages of an open book. If Bella is "Bella Caledonia" then this intertextuality becomes significant for the way in which we read the nation. Bella, like *Poor Things* itself, is a composite creature, stitched together from fragments of texts, cultures and opinions. Is Scotland, then, a composite nation? The different voices that Gray "plagiarises" combine to make a whole. In the very title of his pamphlet *Why Scots Should Rule Scotland*, Gray defines the nation in terms of its citizens, and he specifies that by "Scots" he means "everyone in Scotland who is able to vote" (Gray 1992b: 5). A nation is made up of the multiple voices or votes of its citizens.

Although she is labelled "Bella Caledonia", however, Bella's Scottish identity becomes problematic. In her "Letter to Posterity", Victoria informs us:

My own mother had made me Mancunian. The nuns had made me French. The friendship and conversation of Mrs. Dinwiddie gave me the voice and manners of an unprejudiced, straightforward Scotswoman. Colleagues who knew nothing of my early years still amuse me sometimes by saying how SCOTTISH I am. (Gray 1992a: 261)

She herself mocks the idea that she incarnates an essential Scottish-ness, and also directs the reader back to the "Bella Caledonia" portrait, advising us that "if you ignore the Gainsborough hat and pretentious nickname it shows I am a plain, sensible woman" (251). According to Gray's definition in *Why Scots Should Rule Scotland*, Bella (or Victoria), as citizen, is indeed Scottish as she lives and works in Scotland. Bella (Caledonia) as metaphor for the nation, however, highlights the fact that women representing the nation cannot be citizens – they may contain or mother citizens, but they are not citizens themselves. Therefore, the woman representing the nation is not bound by the same definitions as citizens: Victoria is a Scottish citizen, but Bella as nation does not occupy an unambiguously Scottish body. As McCandless puts it, in his description of Bella on the page opposite the "Bella Caledonia" portrait, "her black hair and eyebrows, sallow skin and bright golden-brown eyes seemed dazzlingly foreign and right..." (Gray 1992a: 44). Like Burns's "outlandish hizzie" from "The Vision", Bella is both foreign *and* right, both citizen and nation, other and home. She is a composite, and a composite made from non-Scottish sources as well as Scottish ones.

## Woman as monster: Liz Lochhead

The woman-as-nation figure is expected to appear and function in a certain way – and yet, it seems, she inevitably ruptures the boundaries which have been set up for her and breaks out of her fixed role. This gap between expectation and reality is a crucial component of what can make her monstrous. The word "monstrous" in *Poor Things*, we saw, describes not appearance but the breaking of natural laws. Things or people become monstrous when they deviate from the normal. But, of course, the definition of what is "normal" depends on the eye of the beholder. It is in this way that the female body becomes associated with the monstrous. If a woman deviates from what is regarded as "normal", transgresses the limits of the roles defined for her – good mother, good wife, good daughter – she becomes monstrous. In *The Madwoman in the Attic*, Sandra Gilbert and Susan Gubar argue that "the images of 'angel' and 'monster' have been so ubiquitous throughout literature by men that they have also pervaded women's writing to such an extent that few women have definitively 'killed' either figure" (Gilbert and Gubar 1979: 17). Female writers' fascination with monster figures is explored in the anthology of Scottish and Irish women's poetry *Sleeping with Monsters* (Wilson and Somerville-Arjat eds 1990). The title comes from Adrienne Rich's *Snapshots of a Daughter-in-Law* (1963) whose title poem includes the lines "A thinking woman sleeps with monsters / The beak that grips her, she becomes". In this collection, the editor states that,

[...] monsters, once we started looking, cropped up everywhere – in how women perceive themselves and how they feel they are perceived, in their actual experience as much as in images from myth or legend or crude stereotype. (Wilson and Somerville-Arjat eds 1990: xvi)

The monstrosity experienced by women writers may be found in the gap between how they perceive themselves and how they feel they are being perceived. Women in literature and in society can become monsters if they do not correspond to the roles expected of them. As Angela Carter wrote in *The Sadeian Woman*, "A free woman in an unfree society will be a monster" (Carter 1979: 27).

In *Blood and Ice*, her play about the writing of *Frankenstein*, Liz Lochhead refers directly to Carter in this speech by her Mary Shelley character:

Oh Freedom in a man may be all very well, but...
A Free Woman is a loose woman.
A Free Woman in the society of the Unfree will be...
A monster.
In an unfree society the worst monster will be a loose woman. (Lochhead 1982: 31)

Like Alasdair Gray, Liz Lochhead draws on *Frankenstein* as a key source for her exploration of the monstrous, and indeed Gray cites Lochhead's *Blood and Ice* as one of his inspirations for *Poor Things*, along with *Ariel Like a Harpy*, Christopher Small's study of *Frankenstein* (Gray 1992a: iv). Lochhead's focus on the monstrous female body is concerned primarily with the role of women in society, rather than the symbolic representation of woman. Her exploration of the idea of the monstrous, however, not only in her dramatic and poetic rewritings of *Frankenstein* but also in her play *Dracula* (1989) and many of her poems which rework fairy tales deal precisely with literary constructions of femininity.

Like Gray, Lochhead mixes Mary Shelley's biography with the plot of *Frankenstein*, paralleling the making of the monster with the way in which Shelley perceived herself to be constructed by her situation and her companions. In Lochhead's play the same actor plays Percy Shelley and Frankenstein, while Byron doubles as the monster. However unlike Gray, Lochhead is particularly concerned with the idea of the female writer as monster. Lochhead also powerfully imagines the genesis of *Frankenstein* as a mixture of literary creation and sexuality in the poem "Dreaming Frankenstein" in the collection of the same name (1984: 11–12). In the introduction to the second edition of *Frankenstein* in 1831, Mary Shelley described her inspiration for *Frankenstein* as "the spectre which haunted [her] midnight pillow" (Shelley [1818] 1996: 172). Lochhead's poem makes this scene of nocturnal inspiration into a passage of pure nightmare horror:

She said she
woke up with him in
her head, in her bed.
Her mother-tongue clung to her mouth's roof
in terror, dumbing her, and he came with a name
that was none of her making. (Lochhead 1984: 11)

The poem ends

Eyes on those high peaks
in the reasonable sun of the morning,
she dressed in damped muslin
and sat down to quill and ink
and icy paper. (12)

In the collection *Sleeping with Monsters*, speaking about her fascination with Mary Shelley, Lochhead says, "Why would Mary Shelley write about monsters? I was haunted by that phrase from Goya: 'The sleep of reason produces monsters.'" (Wilson and Somerville-Arjat eds 1990: 13). In "Dreaming Frankenstein" the sleep of reason is dramatised in the nocturnal encounter with the spectre of the monster, outside the realm of language. Reason and language are reinstated in the cold light of day and allow Mary Shelley to begin writing, and yet having slept with the monster, she can never be rid of him. In the monologue which closes the play *Blood and Ice*, Mary Shelley states:

I am the monster, poor misunderstood creature feared and hated by all mankind. And then I thought: it is worse, worse than that, I am the female monster, gross, gashed, ten times more hideous than my male counterpart, denied life, tied to the monster bed for ever. (Lochhead 1982: 34)

Lochhead's identification of Mary Shelley with the monster is very close to Gilbert and Gubar's reading of the monster, "nameless as a woman in patriarchal society", as a "monstrous Eve":

Women have seen themselves (because they have been seen) as monstrous, vile, degraded creatures, second-comers, and emblems of filthy materiality, even though they have also been traditionally defined as superior beings, angels, better halves. (Gilbert and Gubar 1979: 241; 240)

The political monstrosities that concern Lochhead, then, are primarily gender politics rather than nationalist politics. As she put it herself in an interview, "I still have more of that Scottishness to explore, perhaps because until recently I've felt that my country was woman" (Nicholson 1992: 223). This has echoes of Virginia Woolf's "as a woman I have no country. As a woman, my country is the whole world" (Woolf 1938: 197). However Lochhead adds, "I feel that my country is Scotland as well". And she does extend her feminist analysis of the condition of women in Scotland to the condition of Scotland itself, particularly in her play *Mary Queen of Scots Got Her Head Chopped Off* (1989). Her fascination with the monstrous perhaps allows her to make the transition in this play, as the boundaries between the monstrous female and the monstrous nation become blurred. She does not construct a monstrous Scotland in the same way as Alasdair Gray, however. Focussing on the female figurehead of nation allows her to parallel the ways in which women and nations may be represented. In another interview she claims that "Scotland is like a woman; the Scots know they are perceived from the outside" (quoted in Varty 1997: 642), and this idea of being "perceived from the outside" is connected to monstrosity because the external gaze constructs the monster. Women are perceived from outside in multiple ways, and as we have seen this is one way in which they become monstrous. Like MacDiarmid's Scottish muse, rather than being one thing they become many.

In *Mary Queen of Scots Got her Head Chopped Off* (1989), Scotland is multiple and monstrous from the outset. La Corbie, the "chorus", introduces herself as the "national bird" of Scotland, "black beady een in ma executioner's hood. No braw, but Ah think Ah ha'e a sort of black glamour. [...] I live on lamb's eyes and road accidents" (Lochhead 1989: 11–12). This "ragged, ambiguous creature" describes a Scotland which may be "a peatbog, ... a daurk forest. / It's a cauldron o' lye, a saltpan or a coal mine" (11). Scotland may be rich or poor, light or dark, negatively or positively connoted, depending on your point of view. In Lochhead's play, the queen of Scotland takes on this multiple identity; both Mary Queen of Scots and her political counterpart over the border, Elizabeth I of England, represent their nations as figureheads and both take on something of the monstrous multiplicity of their nations. John Knox famously constructed femininity as monstrous when he denounced the rule of women, particularly Mary Tudor of England and Mary Queen of Scots, in his *First Blast of the Trumpet Against the Monstrous Regiment of Women* (1558), and Lochhead's Knox reminds us of his work in Act 1 Scene 4. What makes the regiment of women monstrous in this play, however, is the gap between role and reality. Both queens are a little bit monstrous because they are stretched to fulfil the expectations of their respective societies. Multiple perceptions of Mary and Elizabeth, who are simultaneously individuals and icons of nation, complicate their iconic status and their relationship to their nations.

The body of Elizabeth, the "Virgin Queen", historically merged the iconography of the head of state with that of the motherland, and she came to represent, in the words of Marina Warner, "both figurehead and ship" (Warner 1996: 42). In Lochhead's play the figures of Elizabeth and Mary shift between symbolic representations of their nations and individual women facing their own emotional problems. The changing faces of both queens is dramatically emphasised by the fact that the actors playing Mary and Elizabeth also play a range of other characters from both ends of the social spectrum. Thus, with a crack of La Corbie's whip, Mary becomes Marian, Elizabeth's serving woman; Mairn, a beggar girl in sixteenth-century Scotland; and Marie, a twentieth-century schoolgirl. Elizabeth, likewise, plays Mary's maid Bessie, Mairn's friend Leezie; and the contemporary child Betty. Like their historical counterparts, the characters Elizabeth and Mary never meet, but the Elizabeth/Mary duality is reproduced through a number of other closer encounters: between Mary and Bessie, in whom Mary confides her anxieties; between Elizabeth and Marian, her concerned maidservant; between Mairn and Leezie; Betty and Marie.

This fragmentation of the names and the figures of the queens illustrates a multiplicity of female roles, and marks the gap between the iconic figurehead of the queen and the individual female body. The "doubles" of the two queens are allowed to express emotions and to behave in ways inappropriate to a queen. As La Corbie says, "when's a queen a queen / And when's a queen juist a wummin?" (16). The beggar child Leezie, admiring Queen Mary in the royal pro- cession, remarks "Mind you, we'd be braw in braw claes" (32). The clothes make the queen, and transform the individual woman into the figurehead. The repeated refrain "Och, when a Queen wad wed / Or tak' a man to bed, / She only does whit ony maid funns chancy" has the double effect of humanising the figurehead and drawing attention to the gap between the figurehead and the human (18; 25). Through all these transformations Elizabeth and Mary retain some essential char- acteristics, however, which they are better able to express as serving- woman or as beggar than as queen.

Lochhead plays, however, with the traditional iconography of both queens. Elizabeth's chaste body represented the security of Eng- land, particularly at the time of the Spanish Armada, as well as guar- anteeing the security of Elizabeth herself on the throne of England. Mary, in Scotland, was in a much more precarious political position, largely due to her position as a Catholic monarch in a Protestant state. Traditionally, in opposition to Elizabeth's closed, secure body, Mary's body is sexualised, and thus both her reign and the situation of Scot- land are represented as unstable and vulnerable to attack. Lochhead refers to this dualism between the bodies of Elizabeth and Mary, but she also complicates it by putting great emphasis on Elizabeth's rela- tionship with Robert Dudley. Whether as Bessie, Betty or Leezie, Elizabeth's character is sensual and sexually knowledgeable, a "tarty wee" girl (32), or a "lewd child" (64). Mary's alter egos, on the other hand, are much more "modest" (17), diffident, and, in the playground scene, victimised.

The beginning of the play sees both Queens being courted by a succession of suitors, and while Mary tells her serving maid, "I want to marry and begin my reign at last" (17), Elizabeth says "I have always said I shall marry – if I marry – as queen and not as Elizabeth" (18). However, Elizabeth's virgin body and Mary's sexualised body become confused. As Elizabeth says, Mary is " a virgin too, although she has been married. Altogether doing it exactly the wrong way round for my taste, but still..." (25). In contrast, Elizabeth's "repressed love" for her favourite, Robert Dudley, Lord Leicester, her lover who she cannot marry, leads her into monstrous dreams about her childhood and her present. In the dream she plays with a doll whose head is off, a reference both to her mother, Anne Boleyn, beheaded by Henry VIII, and to the end of the play, the beheading of Mary.

Mary's body, of course, becomes monstrous in her death, towards which the whole play moves. Several times references are made to Mary's height – Elizabeth says to Marian, "She is too high" (17), and again "Bit on the tall side, of course" (25). Mary's body is mutilated, made monstrous, literally cut down to size, and as the title of the play and the final playground scene show, it is by her death that she is remembered in the popular imagination, in the playground song "Mary Queen of Scots got her head chopped off". If the body of Elizabeth functioned, particularly after her death, as a symbol for the dominance and inviolate borders of England, the body of Mary functions in an unfortunately apt way for the state of Scotland after her death. Metaphorically decapitated, effectively losing her king to England, from 1603 on Scotland is well on the way to becoming the monstrous Scotland that Alasdair Gray describes in *Why Scots Should Rule Scotland*.

## The Caledonian Antisyzygy and other deformed theories

Discussing Liz Lochhead's monsters, S.J. Boyd states that:

> Scotland, indeed, is particularly fertile ground for monsters, mythical, real, and in-between; from Nessie to Morag, from Ian Brady to Dennis Nilsen, from Macbeth (and his Lady) to Sawnie Bean, from Robert Wringhim to Mr Hyde. (Boyd 1994: 40)

Here Boyd taps in to a tradition which, as he acknowledges, can be traced back to Gregory Smith's *Scottish Literature: Character and Influence* (1919). The deformed body of Bella Caledonia may be seen as growing out of the critical history surrounding Smith's phrase "Caledonian antisyzygy", that heavily overused term in Scottish literary studies.

T. S. Eliot, in his review of Smith's book, rather disparagingly titled "Was there a Scottish literature?", saw no value in a provincial literature, and said that Scottish literature as surveyed by Smith lacked coherence, without even having an anchor in a single language (Eliot 1919: 680). But Gregory Smith insisted on the diversity of Scottish literature. He took apart any pretensions Scottish literature had to cohesion, and emphasised its variety and tendency towards doubleness and contrast. He argued that the very basis of Scottish literature could be found in a union of opposites, which he playfully termed "the Caledonian antisyzygy":

Perhaps in the very combination of opposites – what either of the two Thomases, of Norwich and Cromarty, might have been willing to call "the Caledonian antisyzygy" – we have a reflection of the contrasts which the Scot shows at every turn, in his political and ecclesiastical history, in his polemical restlessness, in his adaptability, which is another way of saying that he has made allowance for new conditions, in his practical judgement, which is the admission that two sides of the matter have been considered. If therefore, Scottish history and life are, as an old northern writer said of something else, "varied with a clean contrair spirit," we need not be surprised to find that in his literature the Scot presents two aspects which appear contradictory. Oxymoron was ever the bravest figure, and we must not forget that disorderly order is order after all. (Smith 1919: 45)

The phrase "Caledonian antisyzygy" has an odd status here: parenthetical, in quotation marks and displaced into the ghostly mouths of Thomas Browne and Thomas Urquhart. Its context suggests that the phrase should not be taken for granted. And the spirit of Smith's passage is much closer to Bakhtinian dialogism than to what subsequent critical history has made it: a justification of the representation of Scotland as having some kind of psychological deformity. Smith's generalisations about "the Scot" and his tendency to exhibit contrasts are translated into generalisations about "the Scottish psyche". Scottish critics, following Hugh MacDiarmid who used the phrase most famously in his article "The Caledonian Antisyzygy and the Gaelic Idea" (MacDiarmid [1931–32] 1969a), have used the idea of the "Caledonian antisyzygy" as the basis of a view of Scottish literature which sees it essentially built on splits, schisms and dualities, and, even worse, that Scottish national culture is fundamentally incoherent

and indeed "neurotic". In 1936, Edwin Muir pronounced pessimisti-
cally on the linguistic situation in Scotland, claiming that "the curse of
Scottish literature is the lack of a whole language, which finally means
thc lack of a whole mind" (Muir [1936] 1982: 9).

Tom Nairn, in *The Break-Up of Britain*, writes of nationalism as
"the pathology of modern develomental history, as inescapable as
'neurosis' to the individual" (Nairn 1981: 359), and although there is
nothing specifically Scottish about his claims here, Cairns Craig is
able to expand on Nairn's text, giving it the explicitly Scottish twist
that was implicit in Nairn: "The word 'land' implies a unitary '*Geist*'
that could not exist, but having implied it Nairn can then go in search
of the sickness that afflicts the spirit, the psychoses in the communal
Scottish mind" (Craig 1996: 93). Craig adopts a more dialogical
approach to the relationship between English and Scots, British and
Scottish, in *The Modern Scottish Novel* (1999: 30–31). The notion of
the "schizophrenic Scot" has become almost a commonplace in Scottish literary criticism, although it is generally based on a rather simplified understanding of schizophrenia as "split personality" and which
may therefore personify the splits supposedly inherent in Scottish
culture.

This personification of a troubled mental state is not so far from
the personification of physical deformity in the figure of Bella Caledonia, and, just like Bella's physical deformities, the mental problems
personify two different kinds of "split": internal divisions in Scotland,
particularly linguistic divisions, and Scottishness as opposed to Britishness, which is the split Gray personifies by means of his two-
bodied monster in *Why Scots Should Rule Scotland*. Gray's representation of physical deformity functions similarly to MacDiarmid's and
subsequent Scottish critics' metaphor of mental illness. In either case,
the political disjunction between Scotland and Britain is represented
as illness, in one case of the allegorical body of Scotland, in the other
of the bodies of the Scots. The way in which Gray fictionalises the
deformed body of Scotland in *Poor Things* brings both metaphors
together. Instead of representing Scotland by either a deformed body
or a split mind, Gray emphasises the split between body and mind. So
the "monstrous" anatomical construction of Bella is focused upon her
brain, and this raises several problems, both in the interpretation of the
dual narratives of the story and in its implications for a political reading of the construction of Bella.

The metaphorical distance between Bella's body and brain might refer to the remote government of Scotland, but rather than focusing on the question of government in *Poor Things*, Gray uses Bella to comment on the plight of a country which has lost touch with its sense of history. Early in the novel Bella envies a lady described as "a woman with a past", and says that she will have to acquire "a lot of past fast" (Gray 1992a: 61). Like Frankenstein's monster, her education has to be acquired in other ways, most particularly on the European tour she undertakes during her "elopement" with Wedderburn, during which she learns (among other things) about politics, poverty and sex. In the course of her travels Bella meets a Russian gambler who tells her that "people who care nothing for their country's stories and songs [...] are like people without a past – without a memory – they are half people" (116). Bella, whose infant brain has no memory of her body's earlier life (Baxter has told her that her parents died in a South American railway accident which also caused her amnesia), immediately sees a personal parallel in this: "Imagine how that made me feel! But perhaps, like Russia, I am making up for lost time" (116). In this passage there is an explicit parallel between Bella's lack of past and the national lack of past. The Russian gambler also proposes that a nation is as old as its literature:

"Our literature began with Pushkin, a contemporary of your Walter Scott," he told me. "Before Pushkin Russia was not a true nation, it was an administered region [...] Pushkin learned the folktales from his nursemaid, a woman of the people. His novellas and poems made us proud of our language and aware of our tragic past – our peculiar present – our enigmatic future. He made Russia a state of mind – made it real. [...] But you had Shakespeare centuries before Walter Scott." (Gray 1992a: 115–16)

This suggests that a nation's consciousness can only be as old as its literature, no matter how long it may have existed in statute. If Pushkin "made Russia a state of mind – made it real" then a nation can only be real if it has been imagined. If literature creates a nation's "state of mind" Bella's brain may represent that state of mind contained within her body which is Bella Caledonia, bonnie Scotland, the form of the land itself. As the development of Bella's brain is charted through changes in her writing style, her mind may be the national consciousness, the imagined nation, imagined by a national literature.

Just as Bella's mind is younger than her body, so Scotland's modern national consciousness is younger than the nation and younger than the nation's cultural heritage. But the allegory also works for the state-nation dichotomy. The parliament of an independent Scotland would be much younger than its mother nation, since it has been interrupted for 300 years. The current devolved Scottish parliament is indeed in its infancy and has been transplanted into the body of a mature, post-industrial nation. The connotations of the baby's brain in the adult body are not entirely negative. Bella has an attractive innocence and a political idealism resulting from her lack of social conditioning. She becomes the first female doctor to graduate from Glasgow University, and opens a clinic run on socialist principles, although she is ridiculed by the press. Although the theme of monstrosity suggests political imperfections in Scotland, Bella is not the same kind of monster as the two-necked monster of *Why Scots Should Rule Scotland*. Her social conscience may be read as a potential future for Scotland. Monstrosity is translated into potential. Bella's infant brain may represent "the early days of a better nation" of Gray's recurrent slogan.

## Early days of a better nation?

In an interview Liz Lochhead repeats the "Caledonian Antisyzygy" model of Scottishness, giving it a slight gender twist:

I guess I would say that the big split in Scotland is between self and other self. [...] I think that's natural if you're Scottish when you are half English, really. There's a bit of you who's internalised all of that, so you're English, but you're Scots. So two different halves of you talk to each other which is very similar to the states of the male and the feminine. (Todd 1992: 90; cited in Boyd 1994: 41–42)

As S.J. Boyd comments, Lochhead here "does a fair impersonation" of Lewis Grassic Gibbon's Chris Guthrie (Boyd 1994: 42). Like her "Scotland is like a woman" statement, this goes along the line of equating England with masculinity and Scotland with femininity. This idea of Scots internalising a sense of Englishness is rather like the feminist reader response theory which sees women learning to read as men as a result of reading the work of male authors and critics all their lives (see Schweickart 1986). Lochhead works out the implications of such monstrous splits in *Blood and Ice* and in *Mary Queen of Scots*, but in the end there is no way out of the kind of monstrosity thus constructed. What Gray does in *Poor Things* is to take a tradition of seeing Scotland as essentially divided and transform its allegorical potential into something still monstrous yet potentially positive, reappropriating the celebratory approach to the Caledonian antisyzygy found in Smith and MacDiarmid. As the editor of the collection *Sleeping with Monsters* writes:

Monsters symbolise a fusion of contradictions. [...] The power of monsters is that they jar us out of our own realities. They can scare us, and they can encourage new emotional and conceptual possibilities; they can create, and are created from, both fear and freedom. The woman poet who seeks to name herself and the world around her necessarily sleeps with monsters. (Wilson and Somerville-Arjat eds 1990: xi)

Monsters acquire positive connotations in such a reading: the "fusion of contradictions" is potentially creative and enriching. The deformed body of Bella Caledonia need not necessarily be read negatively. Gray highlights the discourses of monstrosity in the cultural and literary construction of Scotland and proposes an allegorical body in which different constructions of Scotland can co-exist. He opens the door to new narratives of Scotland in which both Scotland and women can be theorised without being critically deformed in the process.

# Chapter Five

## Women Writing Nation

The female personification of Scotland is founded on a series of tensions which, while they make her interesting, perhaps threaten eventually to destroy her from within. These tensions are both formal and ideological. The formal tension has to do with the way in which she is constructed: she is literally deformed – it seems to be impossible to draw one single woman representing Scotland. As the last chapter showed, she is multiple, drawn from a variety of different cultures, and, at the same time, stretched to cover her obligation to represent Scotland both as a nation and as an institution. The ideological tension rests on the fact that among the various female roles on which the woman-as-nation model draws, the most recurrent for the Scottish figure is that of victim. Even if the figure is a strong woman, an Amazon dressed in armour, she is an Amazon waiting to be attacked.

The most significant tension, however, particularly for women writers at the end of the twentieth and beginning of the twenty-first century, is the dichotomy that is set up between nation and citizen. If women function symbolically as the personification of nation, there seems to be no place for them as citizens within their nation, and, by implication, no place for them as writers. The Scotland-as-woman figure, as we have seen, is strangely out of time, even out of place. Emerging seventy-five years after the era of popularity enjoyed by her sisters in England and France, she had no institutional role to play, and, with Irish, English, and continental antecedents, she had no basis in any Scottish historical or literary tradition. She seems to have appeared because she *should* have been there, as part of the necessary paraphernalia of nation, during the Scottish Literary Renaissance, but even then she lacks a definable form. We seem to catch sight of her from the corners of our eyes, in MacDiarmid's muses, in Gibbon's Chris Caledonia, in Gunn's faithful, waiting women, but she is always elusive, always marginal. She emerged, what is more, in a period of nationalism in Scotland which felt the need to assert its virility, and which valorised, in the words of Carol Anderson and Glenda Norquay, the "masculine heroism" of the male nationalist (Anderson and Norquay 1984: 9).

A nationalist literature which makes use of a female personification of the nation asserts a particular kind of nationalism and a particular kind of nation. Nationalist texts which explicitly make use of
the figure of woman as a symbol risk excluding their female readership from the kind of nationalism they represent. As the Irish poet
Eavan Boland has written, discussing the symbolic use of the female
figure in the Irish poetic tradition,

Once the idea of a nation influences the perception of a woman, then that woman is
suddenly and inevitably simplified. She can no longer have complex feelings and
aspirations. She becomes the passive projection of a national idea. (Boland 1996: 136)

This simplification of the figure of woman marginalises women both
as writers and as readers. Women have difficulty locating themselves
in texts which have no space for them except as symbols. Boland
describes the use of the image of woman as nation as a violation of a
necessary ethical relation between imagination and image within Irish
poetry, and documents the process by which she realised she was
assimilating herself both as a nationalist and as a poet into a masculine
poetic tradition which left her no voice to speak. Her answer to the
problem resembles a pledge: "I must be vigilant to write of my own
womanhood [...] in such a way that I never colluded with the simplified images of women in Irish poetry" (Boland 1996: 151–52). Boland
writes that in her experience, it is "easy, and intellectually seductive,
for a woman artist to walk away from the idea of a nation" (Boland
1996: 145). This seems to suggest, however, that the intellectually
seductive path is not necessarily the best way to go, leaving the institutionally and ideologically masculine model of nationalism unchal-
lenged. To ignore the question of nation is certainly one way for
women writers to escape from the "double-cross" (Reizbaum 1992) of
a traditionally androcentric national canon and a male nationalist
ideology. But this is only one model of nationalism, and only one
model of what a nationalist text could be like. There is no reason why
a Scottish writer should be required to engage in this model of nationalism or indeed in nationalism at all, and yet the assumption that there
is a blanket definition of "Scottishness" has hampered Scottish writers
– and perhaps particularly Scottish women writers – throughout the
twentieth century.

## How to be Scottish

Asked by the *Edinburgh Review* what effect a devolved Scottish Parliament would have on Scottish writing, Janice Galloway answered: "On the one hand, of course, a parliament will have no effect whatsoever on Scottish writing ... Writers don't follow politicians, rather the reverse". However on a practical level she hoped that Scotland might follow Ireland's lead in introducing tax concessions for artists, which would encourage other writers and artists to move to Scotland. "Cross-fertilised soil is always richer, and it might help get us off some of the rather tedious single track roads this country's writers are often expected to go down" (Galloway 1999: 72). The single-track was the expectation that Scottish writers, in the late twentieth century, would have something to say about national identity. Scottish literature as a discipline is studied so as to reveal something about Scotland as a nation, and the institutionalised canon has a role to play in determining cultural production and representing a coherent picture of national life. In order to maintain its tenuous position as a distinct discipline in the Scottish academic community, Scottish literature has tended to defend its existence by demonstrating a *difference* from English literature: the influence of a distinct cultural tradition as well as of different languages. Such an attitude to the study of Scottish literature links it, firstly, to the very negative constructions of national identity which define Scotland as "not England", and is in direct contrast to the very catholic scope of most English literature departments. There exists a tendency to justify the existence of Scottish literature by imposing a uniform definition of Scottishness upon texts. The cultural situation of Scotland, we are led to believe, can thus be read from any text purporting to be "Scottish" no matter how much a text might resist such a reading. Dorothy McMillan suggests that:

for contemporary Scottish novelists the nation, its myths and allegories, however monstrous, are probably inescapable... It may be a wish to frustrate the reading of their novels as national allegory that sends Alan Massie and William Boyd and Ronald Frame in flight to Rome or France or Africa or Bath... (McMillan 1995: 81)

This recent determination that there must be an intrinsic "Scottishness" to texts that is not merely geographical but necessarily cultural or political leads to a skewed perspective on recent Scottish writing. Rather like the cloak illustrated with the national landscape worn by the woman-as-nation figure, Scottish writers are required to don a "tartan shawl" of Scottishness (Metzstein 1993: 137). The critical reception of the cultural phenomenon that is the recent wave of Scottish writing tends to involve reading every new narrative of fractured identity, from Janice Galloway's *The Trick is to Keep Breathing* to Irvine Welsh's *Trainspotting*, as an allegory for the political situation of Scotland. This indicates a rather blinkered stance and a disturbing lack of imagination among the Scottish critical community, journalistic and academic, and represents an urge to create an artificial homogeneity within Scottish culture while dismissing the existence of external influences on writers such as Alan Warner and Irvine Welsh.

Discussion of Scottish women's writing is perhaps even more haunted by the spectre of "Scottishness" than discussion of their male counterparts. As the editors of *The History of Scottish Women's Writing* note, the volume provoked the familiar debate as to "what constitutes a 'Scottish' writer or work", in a more extreme form. This could be because, as the editors suggest, the lack of an established canon of Scottish women writers means there is no real benchmark against which to define the Scottishness of individual female writers. The bibliography to the *History* emphasises that "Decisions about inclusion [...] have tended towards openness in the interpretations of Scottishness" (Gifford and McMillan eds 1997: x; 677). Similarly, the editors of *Contemporary Scottish Women Writers* bemoan the fact that Ellen Galford tends not to be considered a Scottish writer due to the "accident of her birth in New Jersey... while many of her concerns, in fact, place her within contemporary Scottish cultural contexts" (Christianson and Lumsden eds 2000: 4). Arguing from the other direction, however, in her chapter "Woman and Nation" in *The History of Scottish Women's Writing*, Susanne Hagemann discusses the collection of short stories *The Other Voice: Scottish Women's Writing Since 1808* (Burgess ed. 1987). Hagemann finds the editorial policy of selection and definition in this volume to be arbitrary and contradictory, commenting that:

> If short stories such as Nancy Brysson Morrison's "No Letters, Please" and Janet Caird's "The Deprived" [...] are typical, then Scottishness does not hold much interest for woman writers. If this is the case, however, the editorial purpose indicated by the word *Scottish* in the collection's subtitle, *Scottish Women's Writing Since 1808*, is self-defeating. (Hagemann 1997: 321)

Ellen Galford is not considered as a Scottish author because of where she happened to be born; yet Hagemann seems to suggest that even if an author is born in Scotland, only an explicit concern with "Scottishness" qualifies her to be described as Scottish. According to this logic women writers do not qualify as "Scottish" if their preoccupations are feminist, or merely concerned with everyday life rather than explicitly with nation or nationalism. This restrictive definition of "Scottishness" implies a narrow and almost necessarily androcentric canon, and it remains difficult for women to write themselves into such a tradition.

Even though, as the editors of the collection *Contemporary Scottish Women Writers* point out, there *were* Scottish women writing in the 1970s and 1980s (Christianson and Lumsden eds 2000: 1), a sense of female exclusion from the dominant Scottish literary scene persisted until at least the mid-eighties. Carol Anderson and Glenda Norquay argued in 1984 that the Scottish Renaissance's violent reaction to the "femininity" of the Kailyard had a legacy which continued late into the twentieth century: "By equating masculinity with Scottishness and taking their models for both from the past, [Scottish men] leave little room for development" (Anderson and Norquay 1984: 9). In *A Drunk Man Looks at the Thistle* (1926) Hugh MacDiarmid effectively opposed women and "Scottishness" in his line "And nae Scot wi' a wumman lies / But I am he..." (MacDiarmid 1987: 78, ll.962–63). Anderson and Norquay argued in 1984 that "by labelling feminism an alternative and a threat to national identity, men make Scottishness their province" (10). While such a patriarchal standpoint may exclude women from Scottishness, a feminist approach may achieve the same thing if Susanne Hagemann is able to suggest that there is something un-Scottish about women not concerned explicitly with the question of nation. Scottish women writers, then, have to escape from both the pigeon-holing of Scottish literary critics and the national narrative which traditionally casts women as "objects which romantically symbolise the nation" (Anderson and Norquay 1984: 10).

Women writers may choose, as Eavan Boland said, "to walk away from the idea of a nation", to ignore the national narrative entirely (Boland 1996: 145). But if they choose in some way to engage with the nation, what possible directions can they go in? In the 1940s Naomi Mitchison attempted to solve the problem by finding a place for herself within the existing masculine tradition, adopting the iconography of nation as woman to the extent of casting herself as the mother of the nation. She abandoned this strategy but did not entirely succeed in rejecting the allegory of woman-as-nation altogether. While her definitions of Scotland and Scottishness were very different from those of, for example, MacDiarmid, Mitchison still subscribed to similar types of gendered myths of nationhood. Other women writing in Scotland, such as those Susanne Hagemann cited from the anthology *The Other Voice*, choose to avoid any overt political concentration on "Scottishness", and focus instead on a specifically female experience which happens, incidentally, to take place within Scotland.

The gender bias of the Scottish Literary Renaissance continues to cast a shadow over Scottish writing today, and women writers still have to cope with masculine constructions of Scottishness in fiction. Scottish writing has attracted greater attention outside Scotland since the mid 1990s. Yet, as Janice Galloway has said, "The word 'Scottish' started to mean this media-thing rather than anything else ... the most visible of it seems to be about being blokey – adolescent blokey at that" (March 2002: 129). Best-sellers such as Irvine Welsh and Iain Banks have set the tone for Scottish fiction, and again women writers do not necessarily fit into the categories that are set up. Ten years earlier, Liz Lochhead articulated a similar frustration: "At the moment I know that I don't like this macho Scottish culture, but I also know that I want to stay here and negotiate it. [...] I can't whinge about it if I don't talk back to it, if I don't have a go" (Nicholson 1992: 223). This notion of "negotiation" with the history of Scottish literature characterises not only Lochhead's work but that of many Scottish women writers trying to situate themselves within the Scottish literary scene. Yet, many women writers in the late twentieth century still feel the need to write back to a dominant "macho" culture which defines perceptions of Scotland both internally and externally. The question is what form this "negotiation" should take. If women writers choose to address questions of national identity, they must find some way of re-inventing the nationalist narrative by re-casting women as agents and citizens within it.

## Rebranding Caledonia

Perhaps the surest way to demonstrate the flaws of the woman-as-nation symbol is to give the symbol a whiff of power. Ellen Galford's *Queendom Come* (1990) contains probably the funniest female incarnation of Scotland in the twentieth century, or indeed at all. In this feminist fantasy, Galford plays with many aspects of the traditional female personification of nation, and in doing so highlights the specific problems faced by a personification of Scotland. Galford's novel begins with the magical resurrection of a tattooed Pictish queen called Albanna on Arthur's Seat on the summer solstice in the late twentieth or early twenty-first century. Albanna returns because she has sworn to awake and help her nation in its hour of need. She is both familiar and unfamiliar as a nation-as-woman figure: armed and Amazon-like, fierce in defence of her nation's rights, yet tattooed and painted with woad, five feet tall and – most unusual – with a mind of her own. *Queendom Come* explores what might happen if a real nation-as-woman figure were actually let loose in the present day, and concludes that the best place for her is safely back in the past.

The problems that Albanna faces are the problems one might expect a female personification of Scotland to encounter. She has been asleep for so long that nobody knows who she is, and the nation that she once ruled has been subsumed into a larger entity. The novel was published in 1990, and the time of need in which Albanna has woken is an indeterminate near future, in, we are told, "the third decade of the Blue Reich" (Galford 1990: 11), where Galford sketches a political satire filled with the projected excesses of the Conservative government. She draws on British cartoonists' common practice of identifying Margaret Thatcher with the figure of Britannia, in breastplate and helmet (Warner 1996: 45): Albanna's martial and autocratic demeanour is paralleled by that of the (never named) female Prime Minister of Great Britain. Indeed the Prime Minister, in an attempt to ingratiate herself with Albanna, introduces herself with a speech in ceremonial blank verse which concludes with the heroic declamation: " I – am – Mother – England!" (61).

Albanna's problem is one of image. The government recognise the marketing potential of this long-dormant symbol – their "all-singing, all-dancing icon of Britain Great Once More" (47). The fact that her name is unfamiliar, and that she was the Queen of Scotland rather than Britain, is unfortunate – "I still wish it had been King Arthur", one of the politicians sighs (41). They try to rebrand her as Boadicea, or, if she prefers, Britannia. As they explain, "You see, Alba – such as it was – is now part of Britain, after all, so it's really nothing more than a sort of modern translation, and...". Albanna, needless to say, is unimpressed by this idea: "If you people had any religious upbringing to speak of, you would know that a name is sacred. You cannot just change it on a whim... any more than you can change a person's sex" (Galford 1990: 42). Nonetheless, the "packaging" of the "product" Albanna is titled "Project Britannia". There is no institutional role for Albanna to play, no longer any Alba for her to represent. Her problem is the same one that has haunted the Scotland-as-woman figure throughout the twentieth century. Without a fixed institutional role, she becomes a free-floating symbol. While the government tries to use her to symbolise their return to old-fashioned values, Scottish nationalists appropriate her for their cause, and the matriarchal structure of her tribe makes her a feminist icon. The trouble is that Albanna refuses to fit any of her images, and once the incumbent government is banished to prehistoric times and she takes over, she proceeds to bring back slavery and military service, and begins plans to invade America (starting with Disneyworld). The high priestess Gwhyldis who brought her out of the past to help her people in their time of need is forced to send her straight back again. Finally, there is no place for her in contemporary society.

Albanna's story aptly illustrates the problems faced by the Scotland-as-woman figure in the twentieth century. She appears anachronistically, brought out of the past into the present day, but with an entire segment of her history missing. She is resurrected for a purpose, but the conflicting expectations of who she will be and how she will behave mean that she never quite works as a symbol.

## Textual Exile: A.L. Kennedy

An alternative version of Scottishness is found in the work of A.L. Kennedy, who offers a very different female perspective on nation, choosing to ignore the problem of gendered national identity as irrelevant and distancing herself from engagement with Scotland. She entirely rejects gendered and symbolic narratives of nation and consistently privileges individual identity over any all-incorporating national identity, thus avoiding the difficulties faced by, for example, Lewis Grassic Gibbon in reconciling the symbolic and the realist in his work. Kennedy explicitly states that "as soon as you start manipulating characters to be examples of all the proletariat, or all Scottishness, they will not be real... You have to create three-dimensional people." She acknowledges the "Scottishness" of her work but rejects any attempt to read it as a nationalist statement: "I use the language that I use, which has Scottishisms, Scottish rhythms in it, but that's not me making a point, that's where I come from" (Merrit 1999: 13). More than this, she attempts to distance herself from any biographical appreciation of her work, saying, "I am a woman, I am heterosexual, I am more Scottish than anything else and I write. But I don't know how these things interrelate" (Kennedy 1995a: 100). Perhaps her most sustained engagement with the question of Scottish identity is the short story "The Role of Notable Silences in Scottish History" which appears in her first volume of short stories, *Night Geometry and the Garscadden Trains* (Kennedy 1990: 62–72). This "explicitly constructionist view of Scottishness" (Hagemann 1997: 325) suggests that all written history is a process of falsehood and fabrication, and that our lives are governed by the lies we are taught to believe about ourselves and our environment. Kennedy thus firmly removes herself from any construction of essential Scottishness, and at the same time tends towards a universal rather than a local moral: "there's no point being Scottish if you can't make up your past as you go along. Everyone else does" (Kennedy 1990: 64). She is aware of the problematic and politicised status of the Scottish writer, and this may account for the marked difference between her earlier work, which is at times overtly concerned with Scottish identity, and her later work, which appears to separate politics and place and elides any overt discussion of the subject of Scottish national identity.

Kennedy's refusal to "manipulate" characters to be "examples of all Scottishness" removes her from the world of the allegorical female figure. Her first novel and earlier collections of short stories, however, deal quite explicitly with issues of national identity. She is also concerned with the role of women in society, but she never uses nationality and gender as metaphors for each other. Rather, in *Looking for the Possible Dance* (1993), and also in her second novel *So I Am Glad* (1995b), her central female characters are citizens of their country, narrating their own stories. Particularly with the figure of Margaret in *Looking for the Possible Dance*, Kennedy is able to break down the binary opposition which demands that nationalists must be male while nations are female, by introducing us to a nationalist daughter with a problematic relation to nation. *Looking for the Possible Dance* describes a journey away from Scotland, although the narrative structure and actual content of the novel are diametrically opposed. The linear narrative sees the protagonist Margaret travel south on a train to London, while the "Scottish" content of the novel (which forms the bulk of it) is contained in memories and flashbacks. Kennedy is thus able to explore, through Margaret, conceptions of what it is to be Scottish, what "Scotland" might be, from a position of increasing physical distance from the object of discussion. The novel illustrates ways in which Scottishness is institutionally constructed by Scots themselves, for example in the summary of Scottish education as "THE SCOTTISH METHOD (FOR THE PERFECTION OF CHILDREN)", enumerated in ten maxims, among them:

2. The history, language and culture of Scotland do not exist. If they did, they would be of no importance and might as well not. [...]
4. The chosen and male shall go forth unto professions while the chosen and female shall be homely, fecund, docile and slightly artistic. [...]
10. Nothing in a country which is nothing, we are defined by what we are not. Our elders and betters are also nothing: we must remember this makes them bitter and dangerous. (Kennedy 1993: 15)

Kennedy here articulates many of the unspoken assumptions lying behind both the problematic definition of "Scottishness" and the sense of exclusion felt by women artists. She also addresses the pervasive sense of victimhood and loss in Scottish nationalism in this description of the ceilidh:

As every languageless, stateless, selfless nation has one last, twisted image of its worst and best, we have the ceilidh. Here we pretend we are Highland, pretend we have mysteries in our work, pretend we have work. We forget our record of atrocities wherever we have been made masters and become comfortable servants again. Our present and past creep in to change each other and we feel angry and sad and Scottish. Perhaps we feel free. (Kennedy 1993: 146)

Kennedy's analysis of Scottishness in *Looking for the Possible Dance* is concerned with constructions of national identity and with the location of the female citizen within this national identity. What is significant is that for most of the book Margaret is physically outside Scotland. Her physical distance from Scotland varies inversely with her mental attachment to her native land so that when she arrives in London she immediately phones Scotland to announce that she is coming back, making her journey in effect a circle. Margaret (perhaps like Kennedy herself) requires the mental vantage point of exile in London in order to properly define Scotland.

The route away from Scotland that Margaret travels in *Looking for the Possible Dance* can be seen as the trajectory governing Kennedy's work in general. In her second collection of short stories, *Now That You're Back* (1994), this exiled vantage point is reproduced several times. In the short story "Friday Payday", a young Scottish prostitute working in London feels homesick, but knows she "wouldn't do this in Glasgow". Her Scotland is a mixture of consumer construction and local knowledge: "adverts on the underground for Scotland, they lied like fuck, but they still made you think" (Kennedy 1994: 142). The girl is aware of the artificial construction of Scotland in the advertisements but her recognition of some sort of truth inherent in the construction marks her own knowledge of Scotland as a safe space. In the same volume, the short story "Christine" sees the (male) Scottish narrator, working in England, articulating a rather different definition of Scottishness. At the outset of the story, he has "chose[n] to be English and disappear", rather, he says, than become either "Rob Roy McStrathspeyandreel or simply [...] Glaswegian" (Kennedy 1994: 15), these being the constructions of Scottishness he perceives as being readable south of the border.

*Now That You're Back* marks a kind of watershed in A.L. Kennedy's treatment of nation and "Scottishness". In her subsequent work the idea of "place" becomes less foregrounded and her explorations of identity become less necessarily connected to national, political identity. One story from the collection in particular illustrates the shift in Kennedy's focus from the explicitly Scottish to the more universal. In *Now That You're Back* the story is published under the title "On Having More Sense" (Kennedy 1994: 29–39), but it was first published, in a slightly different form, as "A Meditation Upon Penguins" in *New Writing Scotland* 10 in 1992. The editors of *New Writing Scotland* describe this earlier version as an example of writers' ability to "refuse to deal with the inverted commas kind of

'Scottishness' and instead examine the old questions in a new way…"
(Galloway and Whyte eds 1992: vii). The basis of the story in both
versions is a preacher-like voice extolling the benefits of taking the
penguin as an example to live life by:

Now perhaps a woman may ask, "How can there truly be untold wonders concealed in
such an unappetising, fishy creature – incapable of even peeling an apple for itself?"
    My answer is as short as the penguin itself. Wonders there are. For is not the
penguin a bird and yet does it not fly in water and not in air, teaching us that all is
possible? (1994: 35)

The humour and the satire on spurious religious rhetoric are present in
both versions and many passages occur in both virtually unchanged.
However the 1992 version of the story explicitly makes the penguin
fable a parable for the situation of Scotland whereas the 1994 version
excises all mention of Scotland and the Scots. Most of the lessons
preached in the first story are tied explicitly to Scottish national identity. The example above, when it occurs in a virtually identical form in
the earlier "A Meditation Upon Penguins", concludes "…teaching us
that all is possible? Even for a Scot" (1992: 79). The injunction, in "A
Meditation Upon Penguins", to "embrace life freely, Scot, and see
how it returns your favour" (1992: 81) is reproduced in "On Having
More Sense" but with the word "Scot" replaced: "embrace life freely,
then […]" (1994: 38). "A Meditation Upon Penguins" culminates
triumphantly with: "Let fly the Penguin Rampant! Let fly all!" (1992:
82) and takes pleasure in forcing the allegory:

Are we not very specially conjoined with the noble creature in choosing, like it, to live
somewhere both movingly picturesque and tragically rich in rheumatic and sinus
complaints? Let our nation take pride not in wealth or domination, but in this (1992:
80).

    By changing a very few words and phrases, Kennedy changes the
story from a spoof Scottish allegory – nation as penguin – to a less
specific, more universal (though still spoof?) message of human understanding towards others. A final two passages illustrate the shift of
narrative intention:

May we, a people at once above and below all other peoples, not learn that there is a
place for us in the great sea of humanity, that we may dive and mingle in it and still

not be lost. Remember, like the penguin, may not a Scot be welcome anywhere? (1992: 78)

Little brothers and sisters, think of the other distances in your lives. Think of the fears you have made into countries and think of the penguin, diving and mingling in ferocious oceans without a boundary or a care. You too may be bold and recognise a place for yourselves anywhere and everywhere in the great sea of humanity. (1994: 34)

Kennedy's later work is more concerned with the individual than the nation, with the "great sea of humanity" than any *specific* nation. "The fears you have made into countries" become of greater concern than a closed focus on Scottish nationalist allegory.

Kennedy's second novel *So I Am Glad* (1995), published one year after *Now That You're Back*, continues her journey away from an explicit concern with Scottishness and national identity. The Scottish setting of the novel is immediately defamiliarised by the fantastic aspect of the plot, the appearance of Savinien de Cyrano de Bergerac in a Glasgow tenement of the 1990s. And while Savinien's naïve questions of Jennifer regarding his surroundings force her to redefine her conception of her personal and political environment, Kennedy's concern is not with questions of national identity. The novel's emotional denouement, if not its actual end, occurs in Paris: the journeys of Kennedy's characters seem to describe her own intellectual movement away from Scotland and Scottish concerns. In her next novel, *Everything You Need* (1999), the move is from civilisation (and Welsh civilisation at that) to individual introspection on a small island inhabited by a writers' commune. And in *Paradise* (2004), the main character Hannah Luckraft travels hopefully all over the world in the hope of finding individual happiness.

Kennedy's progression away from the question of Scottishness represents one possible response for the Scottish woman writer in the twentieth century. Her ability to write about Scotland without resorting to, or even reacting to, tired symbolic constructions of the gendered nation provides an example which suggests that the nation-as-woman figure may have finally exhausted its usefulness for the younger generation of Scottish writers.

## Empty Vessel: Janice Galloway

Unlike Kennedy, Galloway's writing has never dealt with Scottish nationalist issues. Yet like Kennedy's, her fiction, too, moves away from Scotland. Her first novel, *The Trick is to Keep Breathing* (1989), is set in the west of Scotland, but is only concerned with issues of "Scottishness" in passing. *Foreign Parts* (1994), her second novel, follows two Scottish characters, Cassie and Rona, on a holiday touring France. As in *So I Am Glad*, France rather than Scotland becomes a place of self-discovery and realisation. Galloway's third novel, *Clara* (2002), does not deal with Scotland at all, being a fictional biography of Clara Schumann, the concert pianist and wife of the composer Robert Schumann.

Galloway is concerned with the female body, and the iconographic uses to which it may be put, particularly in *The Trick is to Keep Breathing*, where the body of Joy Stone is anatomised and analysed, inside and out, by Joy herself. Joy's depression following the death of her lover Michael leads her to analyse her own life in minute detail, no longer able to distinguish between what is important and what is not. Everything in her life becomes "remarkable" – Joy tells us, "Now I remember everything all the time" (Galloway 1989: 6). Her description of her anorexic and bulimic behaviour and its effects on her body, both outside and inside, give us an image of Joy's body as an object, as well as of Joy as a person. Joy's purging of food from her body emphasises the inside of her body, and its essential "emptiness" (March 1999: 96). That emptiness is vividly illustrated when the doctors insist that Joy has an ultrasound scan, as a result of which she discovers: "I had nothing inside me. The doctor smiled directly at me for the first time. Nothing for either of us to worry about then. Nothing at all" (Galloway 1989: 146). The physical emptiness within Joy recalls the emotional emptiness symbolised in the red "O" of her dead lover's mouth (40), echoed also in the repeated motif of "ooo", which functions as a chapter separator in the novel. In *The Modern Scottish Novel*, Cairns Craig reads Joy's body as a nationalist allegory:

That 'black hole', that 'nothing at all' is the image not only of a woman negated by a patriarchal society but of a society aware of itself only as an absence, a society living, in the 1980s, in the aftermath of its failure to be reborn. (Craig 1999: 199)

As Glenda Norquay points out, Craig's reading of Joy's body here is highly problematic,

> [...] a manoeuvre little different from the interpellation of Chris Caledonia in Lewis Grassic Gibbon's *A Scots Quair*, yet another act of appropriation whereby both the body of the text and that in the text become representative of the motherland. (Norquay 2000: 137)

Rather like Douglas Dunn, Craig at this moment falls prey to the critical tendency to read any Scottish woman, real or fictional, as a potential incarnation of Scotland. There is really nothing in the novel to encourage such a symbolic reading of Joy. However, her anorexia and the absence within her do link her to the allegorical female body, even if only negatively.

The allegorical potential of the anorexic female body has been discussed by Edna Longley in her article "From Cathleen to Anorexia: the breakdown of Irelands". She comments on Paul Muldoon's personification of Anorexia in his poem "Aisling" on the hunger strikes, and suggests that perhaps Anorexia should replace Cathleen ni Houlihan as a female symbol, not of the Irish nation, since "feminists question any exploitation of the female body for symbolic or abstract purposes" but of Irish women themselves, "starved and repressed by patriarchies like Unionism, Catholicism, Protestantism, Nationalism" (Longley 1994: 173). This shifts the object of symbolism but remains a symbolic use of the female body. Joy's anorexia could be read as symbolic of Scottish women in general, "struggling in a male-dominated West of Scotland" (Gifford et al. eds 2002: 732), and certainly the discourses she digests, from the media and from the various forms of authority she encounters, address a wider audience. However Joy cannot be said to symbolise the condition of Scottish women generally. "It is too easy", as Glenda Norquay remarks, "to see Joy as representative of any particular kind of Scottishness, or Scotland" (Norquay 2000: 137). Yet although Joy is not symbolic of Scotland or of the Scottish woman, the emphasis placed on the space inside her, and the contrast between the internal and the external, can encourage us to read her body as an analysis and a criticism of the way in which the female body can be used symbolically. Paradoxically, her body is symbolic of the breakdown of the symbolic female body.

As Joy narrates the minutiae of her life she is very concerned with externals: both appearances and actions. She worries about the mask which defines what she is, the face she presents to society, in the sense both of the face she paints on with make-up, and of the various roles she plays. A major theme of the novel is the examination of the different roles women are required to play in society, a notion that is highlighted by the drama scripts Joy uses to recount conversations. In these conversations she takes the role of "patient" when speaking to a health visitor or doctor (21; 50), "employee" when speaking to her boss (74), and "harridan" with her ex-boyfriend (213). The women's magazines she reads give her a plethora of roles to follow: good mother, successful housewife, ideal lover. Joy feels defined by the various roles society offers her: "This is my workplace", she tells us, "This is where I earn my definition, the place that tells me what I am" (11). Joy's problems centre on the fact that she cannot be defined, that none of the roles offered to her seem sufficient.

Joy constructs her external image carefully. In "The Bathing Ritual" we see her shaving her legs, moisturising ("to keep in the juice"), and putting on make-up: "I tint myself Peaches and Dream, stain my eyelids lilac, brush the lashes black. I smear my lips with clear wax from a stick" (47–48). As Cristie Leigh March puts it, Joy is creating a shell for herself (March 1999: 96). The outside of her body is brittle and painted, contrasted vividly with the visceral reality of the inside, described metonymically in the scene with the soup-can where Joy decides to stop eating. Opening a can of soup for her dinner, Joy accidentally touches the contents of the can: "It felt slimy, unpleasant. Inside the can the surface was a kind of flattened jelly, dark red with bits of green and yellow poking through. Watery stuff like plasma started seeping up the sides of the viscous block." Joy's revulsion at this organic matter appears to lead directly to her revelation: "I didn't need to eat" (Galloway 1989: 38). Joy empties her body literally by refusing to eat and vomiting when she does. Eating is an error, however, and vomiting an emergency measure (87) – her ideal is for her body to be empty inside. As Joy tells us: "It was me who had no substance, nothing under the skin" (175).

The painted, external shell of Joy's body, containing empty space and nothingness, resembles the shell of the symbolic female figure described by Marina Warner. While Joy is certainly, on one level, a portrait of a psychologically realistic character, at the same time her body is anatomised, much more clinically than the body of Bella (Caledonia) Baxter in *Poor Things*. While Gray's *Frankenstein* narrative and anatomical drawings call attention to the gap between Bella's outward appearance and monstrous internal construction, Galloway's much more detailed descriptions of the surface texture of the skin and the way it can be disguised – the blood that leaks when the skin is pierced, and the visceral insides of the body, to be expelled if possible – give a far more disturbing vision of the female body, at the same time familiar and distorted. Bella Caledonia, in comparison, is a cartoon – Joy's body demonstrates what happens when a flesh and blood woman is turned into a shell. The outside of her body becomes tougher: "Diet for a firmer new you!" (27). As she loses weight, she stops menstruating: her body is becoming the reinforced, closed, sealed, sound vessel of the symbolic female figure, and it only leaks (vomiting, self-mutilation) when she loses control.

But Joy is an empty vessel: there is nothing for her to embody. Cairns Craig suggested that her emptiness symbolised Scotland's absence of nationhood, but rather, I would argue, it represents the obsolescence of the various contradictory roles with which she tries to fill her life. Her inner emptiness is connected with her failure to adopt any of the roles she is offered. Outward appearance and inner space are connected, as with the symbolic female figure, who requires only to be dressed in the cloak representing the nation's landscape, and suddenly she *is* the spirit of Scotland. Or she holds a pair of scales and becomes the incarnation of justice. The woman-as-vessel contains the abstract idea, and her outward appearance is adjusted to illustrate it. The roles Joy tries to adopt are all roles that have been used in the construction of the woman-as-nation figure: good housewife, sexually attractive lover, even victim. The significance is not in the fact that Joy shares these roles with the nation-figure, but rather that all of these are staple patriarchal stereotypes of the female. The woman-as-nation figure is founded upon such roles, all of which, like Joy's imagined play-scripts, cast her in relation to a male figure. So she may be a mother, embracing her male citizen-children, or a wife/mistress, possessed by her male citizen-lover. Most problematically, perhaps, she may be a victim, needing to be defended by her male citizen-protector. Joy collapses under the pressure of the roles she is expected to perform, and so, in the end, does the Scotland-as-woman figure.

## End of an old song

Both A.L. Kennedy and Janice Galloway seem to have broken out of the gendered structures of Scottish literature that preceded them. Galloway makes visible the bodies of actual women, and although the sight may be uncomfortable, the bodies she shows us are not distorted like the bodies of Alasdair Gray's women. Nor are they the products of male imagination. Through his pornographic fantasies and his *Frankenstein* narrative, Alasdair Gray highlights the fact that the allegorical female body is generally a male construction. Gray's commentary on the use of the female body to personify the nation in *1982, Janine* and *Poor Things* is the most important in twentieth-century Scottish literature. By satirising the allegory he brings to light many of the weaknesses in the symbolic female figures of the writers of the Scottish Renaissance, particularly MacDiarmid, whose texts he refers to explicitly. Women writers of the Scottish Literary Renaissance, such as Willa Muir and Naomi Mitchison, used the symbolic template established by other writers of the period, and by invoking the Scotland-as-woman figure highlighted the problems she created, both for the representation of actual Scottish women, and for the female artist who could not work within such a symbolic structure. By the end of the twentieth century, and continuing into the twenty-first, however, women writers no longer feel the need to work within the constrictive system of gendered nationalist literature. Galloway and Kennedy are no longer haunted by the spectre of the Scotland-as-woman figure. They are very different types of writer, but both in their different ways move away from traditional constructions of both Scotland and the Scottish woman. Most importantly, perhaps, they are able to break away from the idea that being a Scottish writer requires a particular subject-matter or style. As Janice Galloway wrote on the eve of Scottish devolution in 1999, "Who wants to write about *nation* all the bloody time?" (Galloway 1999: 72).

# Bibliography

Agulhon, Maurice. 1979. *Marianne au combat: l'imagerie et la symbolique républicaines de 1789 à 1880*. Paris: Flammarion.

—. 1989. *Marianne au pouvoir: l'imagerie et la symbolique républicaines de 1880 à 1914*. Paris: Flammarion.

Anderson, Benedict. [1983] 1991. *Imagined Communities: Reflections on the Origin and Spread of Nationalism*. London: Verso.

Anderson, Carol. 1985. *The Representation of Women in Scottish Fiction: Character and Symbol*. PhD thesis. University of Edinburgh.

Anderson, Carol, and Aileen Christianson (eds). 2000. *Scottish Women's Fiction 1920s to 1960s: Journeys into Being*. East Linton: Tuckwell Press.

Anderson, Carol, and Glenda Norquay. 1983. "Interview with Alasdair Gray" in *Cencrastus* 13: 6–10.

—. 1984. "Superiorism" in *Cencrastus* 15: 8–10.

Ashcroft, Bill et al. 1989. *The Empire Writes Back: Theory and Practice in Post-Colonial Literatures*. London and New York: Routledge.

Atwood, Margaret. 1972. *Survival: A Thematic Guide to Canadian Literature*. Toronto: House of Anansi Press.

Barkan, Leonard. 1975. *Nature's Work of Art: The Human Body as Image of the World*. New Haven and London: Yale University Press.

Barker, Elspeth. 1991. *O Caledonia*. London: Penguin.

Berec, Laurent. 2000. "Femininity and Nationalism in Michael Drayton's *Poly-Olbion*". Paper presented at ESSE-5 (Helsinki, 25–29 August 2000).

Boland, Eavan. 1996. *Object Lessons: The Life of the Woman and the Poet in our Time*. London: Vintage.

Boyd, S.J. 1991. "Black Arts: *1982, Janine* and *Something Leather*" in Crawford, Robert and Thom Nairn (eds) *The Arts of Alasdair Gray*. Edinburgh: Edinburgh University Press. 108–23.

—. 1994. "The Voice of Revelation: Liz Lochhead and Monsters" in Crawford, Robert and Anne Varty (eds) *Liz Lochhead's Voices*. Edinburgh: Edinburgh University Press. 38–56.

Burgess, Moira (ed.) 1987. *The Other Voice: Scottish Women's Writing since 1808*. Edinburgh: Polygon.

Burness, Catriona. 1994. "Drunk Women Don't Look at Thistles: Women and the SNP, 1934–94" in *Scotlands* 2: 131–54.

Burns, Robert. 1969. *Poems and Songs* (ed. James Kinsley). Oxford: Oxford University Press.

Burton, Deirdre. 1984. "A Feminist Reading of Lewis Grassic Gibbon's *A Scots Quair*" in Hawthorn, Jeremy (ed.) *The British Working-Class Novel in the Twentieth Century*. London: Edward Arnold. 35–46.

Butler, Judith. 1990. *Gender Trouble*. London and New York: Routledge.

Calder, Jenni. 1997. *The Nine Lives of Naomi Mitchison*. London: Virago.

Camden, William. 1607. *Britannia*. London: Bishop and Norton.

Carlyle, Thomas. [1831] 1987. *Sartor Resartus*. Oxford: Oxford University Press.

Carr, Helen. 1985. "Woman/Indian: 'The American' and his Others" in Barker, Francis et al. (eds) *Europe and Its Others*. 2 vols. Colchester: University of Essex. 2: 46–60.

Carter, Angela. 1979. *The Sadeian Woman: An Exercise in Cultural History*. London: Virago.

Chapman, Malcolm. 1978. *The Gaelic Vision in Scottish Culture*. London: Croom Helm.

Christianson, Aileen, and Alison Lumsden (eds). 2000. *Contemporary Scottish Women Writers*. Edinburgh: Edinburgh University Press.

Corkery, Daniel. [1924] 1967. *The Hidden Ireland: A Study of Gaelic Munster in the Eighteenth Century*. Dublin: Gill and MacMillan.

Cowan, Edward J., and Douglas Gifford (eds). 1999. *The Polar Twins*. Edinburgh: John Donald.

Craig, Cairns (ed.). 1996. *Out of History: Narrative Paradigms in Scottish and British Culture*. Edinburgh: Polygon.

—. 1999. *The Modern Scottish Novel: Narrative and the National Imagination*. Edinburgh: Edinburgh University Press.

Crawford, Thomas. 1989. "The View from the North: Region and Nation in *The Silver Darlings* and *A Scots Quair*" in Draper, R.P. (ed.) *The Literature of Region and Nation*. London: MacMillan. 108–24.

Cruickshank, Helen B. 1962. "Mainly Domestic: Being Some Personal Reminiscences" in Duval, K.D. and S.G. Smith (eds) *Hugh MacDiarmid: A Festschrift*. Edinburgh: K.D. Duval. 187–95.

Cullingford, Elizabeth Butler. 1993. *Gender and History in Yeats's Love Poetry*. Cambridge and New York: Cambridge University Press.

Cusack, Tricia and Síghle Bhreathnach-Lynch (eds). 2003. *Art, Nation and Gender: Ethnic Landscapes, Myths, and Mother-Figures*. Aldershot and Burlington, VT: Ashgate.

Daniels, Stephen. 1993. *Fields of Vision: Landscape Imagery and National Identity in England and the United States*. Cambridge: Polity Press.

Davies, Charlotte Aull. 1996. "Nationalism: Discourse and Practice" in Charles, Nickie and Felicia Hughes-Freeland (eds) *Practicing Feminism: Identity, Difference, Power*. London and New York: Routledge. 156–79.

de Certeau, Michel. 1988. *The Writing of History*. New York: Columbia University Press.

Diamond, Sara. 1985. "Pornography: Image and Reality" in Burstyn, Varda (ed.) *Women Against Censorship*. Vancouver: Douglas and McIntyre. 40–57.

Dickson, Beth. 1987a. "Foundations of the Modern Scottish Novel" in Craig, Cairns (ed.) *The History of Scottish Literature, Volume 4: Twentieth Century*. Aberdeen: Aberdeen University Press. 49–60.

—. 1987b. "From Personal to Global: The Fiction of Naomi Mitchison" in *Chapman*, 10(1–2): 34–40.

Dixon, Keith. 1990. "Rough Edges: The Feminist Representation of Women in the Writing of Lewis Grassic Gibbon" in Schwend, Joachim and Horst Drescher (eds) *Studies in Scottish Fiction in the Twentieth Century*. Frankfurt: Peter Lang. 289–301.

Donne, John. 1971. *The Complete English Poems* (ed. A.J. Smith). Harmondsworth: Penguin.

Donnerstein, Edward. 1988. "An Outline of the Research" in *Pornography and Sexual Violence: Evidence of the Links*. London: Everywoman. 11–24.

Drayton, Michael. 1612–22. *Poly-Olbion: A Choreographicall Description of Great Britain*. London: M. Lownes, I. Browne, I. Helme, I. Busbie.

Dresser, Madge. 1989. "Britannia" in Samuel, Raphael (ed.) *Patriotism: The Making and Unmaking of British National Identity, Volume 3: National Fictions.* London and New York: Routledge. 26–49.

Dunn, Douglas. 1994. "The Representation of Women in Scottish Literature" in *Scotlands* 2: 1–23.

Eliot, T. S. 1919. "Was there a Scottish literature?" in *The Athenaeum* (1 August 1919). 680.

Enloe, Cynthia. 1993. *The Morning After: Sexual Politics at the End of the Cold War.* Berkeley: University of California Press.

Frye, Northrop. [1957] 1971. *Anatomy of Criticism: Four Essays.* Princeton: Princeton University Press.

Galford, Ellen. 1990. *Queendom Come*. London: Virago.

Galloway, Janice. 1989. *The Trick is to Keep Breathing*. Edinburgh: Polygon.

—. and Hamish Whyte (eds). 1992. *Pig Squealing: New Writing Scotland 10*. Aberdeen: ASLS.

—. 1994. *Foreign Parts*. London: Jonathan Cape.

—. 1999. "Poets' Parliament" in *The Edinburgh Review* 100: 71–72.

—. 2002. *Clara*. London: Jonathan Cape.

Gellner, Ernest. 1983. *Nations and Nationalism*. Oxford: Blackwell.

Gibbon, Lewis Grassic (James Leslie Mitchell). [1934] 1967. "Clay" in *A Scots Hairst: Essays and Short Stories* (ed. Ian S. Munro). London: Hutchison. 16–27.

—. [1932–34] 1995. *A Scots Quair*. Edinburgh: Canongate.

Gifford, Douglas. 1987. "Private Confessions and Public Satire in the Fiction of Alasdair Gray" in *Chapman* 50–51: 101–16.

—. and Dorothy McMillan (eds). 1997. *A History of Scottish Women's Writing.* Edinburgh: Edinburgh University Press.

—. et al. (eds). 2002. *Scottish Literature: in English and Scots*. Edinburgh: Edinburgh University Press.

—. and Alan Riach (eds). 2004. *Scotlands: poets and the nation*. Manchester: Carcanet; Edinburgh: The Scottish Poetry Library.

Gilbert, Sandra M., and Susan Gubar. 1979. *The Madwoman in the Attic: The Woman Writer and the Nineteenth-Century Literary Imagination*. New Haven and London: Yale University Press.

Gittings, Christopher E. 1995. "Re-Figuring Imperialism: Gray, Cohen, Atwood and the Female Body" in *The Glasgow Review* 3: 24–36.

Graves, Robert. [1948] 1961. *The White Goddess: A Historical Grammar of Poetic Myth*. London: Faber and Faber.

Gray, Alasdair. 1981. *Lanark: A Life in Four Books*. Edinburgh: Canongate.

—. 1983. *Unlikely Stories, Mostly*. Edinburgh: Canongate.

—. 1984. *1982, Janine*. London: Cape.

—. 1992a. *Poor Things*. London: Bloomsbury.

—. 1992b. *Independence: Why Scots Should Rule Scotland*. Edinburgh: Canongate.

—. 1997. *Why Scots Should Rule Scotland 1997: A Carnaptious History of Britain from Roman Times Until Now*. Edinburgh: Canongate.

—. 2000. *The Book of Prefaces: A Short History of Literate Thought in Word by Great Writers of Four Nations from the 7th to the 20th Century.* London and New York: Bloomsbury.

Gunn, Neil. 1934. *Butcher's Broom.* Edinburgh: Porpoise Press.

—. [1937] 1991. *Highland River.* Edinburgh: Canongate.

Hagemann, Susanne. 1991. *Die Schottische Renaissance: Literature und Nation im 20. Jahrhundert.* Frankfurt: Peter Lang.

—. 1994. "A Feminist Interpretation of Scottish Identity" in *Proceedings of the Scottish Workshop of the ESSE Conference, Bordeaux 1993.* Grenoble: Etudes Ecossaises. 79–91.

—. 1997. "Woman and Nation" in Gifford, Douglas and Dorothy McMillan (eds) *A History of Scottish Women's Writing.* Edinburgh: Edinburgh University Press. 316–28.

Hart, Francis R. 1987. "Neil Gunn's Drama of the Light" in Craig, Cairns (ed.) *The History of Scottish Literature, Volume 4: Twentieth Century.* Aberdeen: Aberdeen University Press. 87–102.

Harvie, Christopher. 1991. "Nationalism, Journalism and Cultural Politics" in Gallagher, Tom (ed.) *Nationalism in the Nineties.* Edinburgh: Polygon. 29–45.

—. 2002. "Ballads – or Blues – of the Nation?" in *Scotland 1802–2002: Figures, Ideas, Formations. Edinburgh Review* 110: 19–35.

Hendry, Joy. 1987. "A Double Knot on the Peeny" in Chester, Gail and Sigrid Nelson (eds) *In Other Words: Writing as a Feminist.* London: Hutchison. 36–45.

Hobbes, Thomas. [1651] 1996. *Leviathan* (ed. Richard Tuck). Cambridge: Cambridge University Press.

Hobsbawm, Eric, and Terence Ranger (eds). 1983. *The Invention of Tradition.* Cambridge: Cambridge University Press.

Hobsbawm, E.J. 1990. *Nations and Nationalisms.* Cambridge: Cambridge University Press.

hooks, bell. 1984. *Feminist Theory from Margin to Center.* Boston: South End Press.

Jayawardena, Kumari. 1986. *Feminism and Nationalism in the Third World.* London and New Jersey: Zed Books Ltd.

Johnson, Toni O'Brien, and David Cairns (eds). 1991. *Gender in Irish Writing.* Milton Keynes and Philadelphia: Open University Press.

Kennedy, A.L. 1990. *Night Geometry and the Garscadden Trains.* Edinburgh: Polygon.

—. 1992. "A Meditation Upon Penguins" in Galloway, Janice and Hamish Whyte (eds) *Pig Squealing: New Writing Scotland 10.* Aberdeen: ASLS. 78–82.

—. 1993. *Looking for the Possible Dance.* London: Secker and Warburg.

—. 1994. *Now that You're Back.* London: Cape.

—. 1995a. "Not Changing the World" in Bell, Ian A. (ed.) *Peripheral Visions: Images of Nationhood in Contemporary British Fiction.* Cardiff: University of Wales Press. 100–2.

—. 1995b. *So I Am Glad.* London: Cape.

—. 1999. *Everything You Need.* London: Cape.

—. 2004. *Paradise.* London: Cape.

Kerrigan, Catherine. 1994a. "Desperately Seeking Sophia" in *Scotlands* 2: 155–63.

—. 1994b. "Nationalism and Gender: Scottish Myths of the Female" in *Proceedings of the Scottish Workshop of the ESSE Conference, Bordeaux 1993*. Grenoble: Etudes Ecossaises, 1994. 105–11.

Kiberd, Declan. 1996. *Inventing Ireland: The Literature of the Modern Nation*. London: Vintage.

Kolodny, Annette. 1975. *The Lay of the Land: Metaphor as Experience and History in American Life and Letters*. Chapel Hill: University of North Carolina Press.

Kreis, Georg. 1991. *Helvetia – Im Wandel der Zeiten: Die Geschichte einer nationalen Repräsentationsfigur*. Zurich: Neue Zürcher Zeitung.

Landes, Joan B. 2001. *Visualising the Nation: Gender, Representation and Revolution in Eighteenth-Century France*. Ithaca and London: Cornell University Press.

Lant, Antonia. 1996. "Prologue: Mobile Femininity" in Gledhill, Christine and Gillian Swanson (eds) *Nationalising Femininity: Culture, Sexuality and British Cinema in the Second World War*. Manchester and New York: Manchester University Press. 13–32.

Lochhead, Liz. 1982. *Blood and Ice*. Edinburgh: Salamander Press.

—. 1984. *Dreaming Frankenstein and Collected Poems*. Edinburgh: Polygon.

—. 1989. *Mary Queen of Scots got her Head Chopped Off* and *Dracula*. Harmondsworth: Penguin.

Lodge, David. 1984. "Sex and Loathing in Scotland" in *The New Republic* 191(19). 43–45.

Longley, Edna. 1994. *The Living Stream: Literature and Revisionism in Ireland*. Newcastle-upon-Tyne: Bloodaxe.

Lorde, Audre. 1984. *Sister Outsider*. Freedom, Calif.: The Crossing Press.

MacDiarmid, Hugh (Christopher Murray Grieve). [1931–32] 1969a. "The Caledonian Antisyzygy and the Gaelic Idea" in Glen, Duncan (ed.) *Selected Essays of Hugh MacDiarmid*. London: Cape. 56–74.

—. [1953] 1969b. "Towards a Celtic Front" in Glen, Duncan (ed.) *Selected Essays of Hugh MacDiarmid*. London: Cape. 171–76

—. [1943] 1972. *Lucky Poet: A Self-Study in Literature and Political Ideas*. London: Cape.

—. 1985. *The Complete Poems of Hugh MacDiarmid* (ed. Michael Grieve and W.R. Aitken). 2 vols. Harmondsworth: Penguin.

—. [1926] 1987. *A Drunk Man Looks at the Thistle* (ed. Kenneth Buthlay). Edinburgh: Scottish Academic Press.

MacGill-Eain, Somhairlle. 1943. *Dàin do Eimhir*. Glasgow: Uilleam MacGhill Fhaolain.

March, Cristie L. 1999. "Interview with Janice Galloway, Glasgow, March 21, 1999" in *Edinburgh Review* 101: 85–98.

—. 2002. *Rewriting Scotland: Welsh, McLean, Warner, Banks, Galloway and Kennedy*. Manchester: Manchester University Press.

McCarey, Peter. 1987. *Hugh MacDiarmid and the Russians*. Edinburgh: Scottish Academic Press.

McClintock, Anne. 1995. *Imperial Leather: Race, Gender and Sexuality in the Colonial Context*. London and New York: Routledge.

McCulloch, Margery. 1987. *The Novels of Neil M. Gunn: A Critical Survey*. Edinburgh: Scottish Academic Press.

McMillan, Dorothy. 1995. "Constructed out of Bewilderment: Stories of Scotland" in Bell, Ian A. (ed.) *Peripheral Visions: Images of Nationhood in Contemporary British Fiction*. Cardiff: University of Wales Press. 80–102.

—. 1997. "Twentieth-Century Poetry I: Rachel Annand Taylor to Veronica Forrest-Thomson" in Gifford, Douglas and Dorothy McMillan (eds). *A History of Scottish Women's Writing*. Edinburgh: Edinburgh University Press. 428–43

Merrit, Stephanie. 1999. "The Books Interview: A.L. Kennedy" in *Observer Review* (25 May 1999). 13.

Metzstein, Margery. 1993. "Of Myths and Men: Aspects of Gender in the Fiction of Janice Galloway" in Wallace, Gavin and Randall Stevenson (eds) *The Scottish Novel Since the Seventies. Edinburgh: Edinburgh University Press*. 136–46.

Mitchison, Naomi. 1947. *The Bull Calves*. London: Cape.

—. 1978. *The Cleansing of the Knife and Other Poems*. Edinburgh and Vancouver: Canongate.

—. 1985. *Among You Taking Notes...: The Wartime Diary of Naomi Mitchison 1939–45* (ed. Dorothy Sheridan). London: Gollancz.

Montrose, Louis. 1993. "The Work of Gender in the Discourse of Discovery" in Greenblatt, Stephen (ed.) *New World Encounters*. Berkeley: University of California Press. 177–217.

Morton, Brian. 1980. "Lewis Grassic Gibbon and the Heroine of *A Scots Quair*" in *EDDA: Nordisk Tidsskrift for Litteraturfarskning* 4: 193–203.

Muir, Willa. [1936] 1996a. *Mrs Grundy in Scotland* in *Imagined Selves* (ed. Kirsty Allen). Edinburgh: Canongate.

—. [1936] 1996b. "Women in Scotland" in *Imagined Selves* (ed. Kirsty Allen). Edinburgh: Canongate.

Murray, Isobel. 1987. "Novelists of the Renaissance" in Craig, Cairns (ed.) *The History of Scottish Literature, Volume 4: Twentieth Century*. Aberdeen: Aberdeen University Press. 103–17

Murray, Stuart and Alan Riach (eds). 1995. *Celtic nationalism and postcoloniality*. SPAN, 41.

Nairn, Tom. [1977] 1981. *The Break-Up of Britain: Crisis and Neo-Nationalism*. London: Verso.

Nicholson, Colin. 1992. "Liz Lochhead: The Knucklebones of Irony" in *Poem, Purpose and Place: Shaping Identity in Contemporary Scottish Verse*. Edinburgh: Polygon. 202–23.

Norquay, Glenda. 2000. "Janice Galloway's Novels: Fraudulent mooching" in Christianson, Aileen, and Alison Lumsden (eds) *Contemporary Scottish Women Writers*. Edinburgh: Edinburgh University Press, 2000. 131–43.

Paisley, Janet. 1999. "Scots Wha Hinnae to Scots Wha Hae: A Road Movie for the Page" in *Edinburgh Review* 100: 74–77.

Parker, Andrew et al. (eds). 1992. *Nationalisms and Sexualities*. New York and London: Routledge.

Plain, Gill. 1996. *Women's Fiction of the Second World War: Gender, Power and Resistance*. Edinburgh: Edinburgh University Press.

*Pornography and Sexual Violence: Evidence of the Links*. London: Everywoman, 1988.

Price, Richard. 1991. *The Fabulous Matter of Fact: The Poetics of Neil M. Gunn*. Edinburgh: Edinburgh University Press.

Reizbaum, Marilyn. 1992. "Canonical Double-Cross: Scottish and Irish Women's Writing" in Lawrence, Karen K. (ed.) *Decolonising Tradition: New Views of Twentieth Century "British" Literary Canons*. Urbana and Chicago: University of Illinois Press. 165–90.

Richardson, Thomas C. 1989. "Reinventing Identity: Nationalism in Modern Scottish Literature" in Drescher, Horst W. and Hermann Völkel (eds) *Nationalism in Literature: Third International Scottish Studies Symposium Proceedings*. Frankfurt am Main: Peter Lang. 117–29.

Rose, Gillian. 1993. *Feminism and Geography*. Minneapolis: University of Minnesota Press.

Ross, Alexander. [1778] 1938. "Helenore, or The Fortunate Shepherdess 1778" in *The Scottish Works of Alexander Ross, M. A.* (ed. Margaret Wattle). Edinburgh: Blackwood. 9–141.

Sampson, Anthony. 1962. *Anatomy of Britain*. New York: Harper and Row.

Samuel, Raphael (ed.) 1989. *Patriotism: The Making and Unmaking of British National Identity, Volume 3: National Fictions*. London and New York: Routledge.

Sasson, Jean P. 1991. *The Rape of Kuwait: The True Story of Iraqui Atrocities Against a Civilian Population*. New York: Knightsbridge.

Schama, Simon. 1995. *Landscape and Memory*. London: Fontana.

Schoene, Bertholdt. 1995. "A Passage to Scotland: Scottish Literature and the British Post-Colonial Condition" in *Scotlands* 2(1): 107–31.

Schweickart, Patrocinio P. 1986. "Reading Ourselves: Towards a Feminist Theory of Reading" in Flynn, Elizabeth A. and Patrocinio P. Schweickart (eds) *Gender and Reading: Essays on Readers, Texts and Contexts*. Baltimore and London: John Hopkins University Press. 31–62.

Scott, Walter. 1899. *The Poetical Works of Sir Walter Scott*. Edinburgh: Sands and Co.

Sedgwick, Eve Kosofsky. [1993] 1994. *Tendencies*. London: Routledge.

Shelley, Mary. [1818] 1996. *Frankenstein* (ed. J. Paul Hunter). New York and London: Norton Critical Edition.

Showalter, Elaine. 1977. *A Literature of Their Own: British Women Novelists from Brontë to Lessing*. Princeton: Princeton University Press.

Small, Christopher. 1972. *Ariel Like a Harpy: Shelley, Mary and Frankenstein*. London: Gollancz.

Smith, Anthony. 1971. *Theories of Nationalism*. London: Duckworth.

—. 1987. *The Ethnic Origins of Nations*. Oxford and New York: Blackwell.

Smith, G. Gregory. 1919. *Scottish Literature: Character and Influence*. London: MacMillan.

Smith, Stevie. 1985. *The Collected Poems of Stevie Smith*. Harmondsworth: Penguin.

Stirling, Kirsten. 1999. "'The Roots of the Present': Naomi Mitchison, Agnes Mure MacKenzie and the Construction of History" in Cowan, Edward J. and Douglas Gifford (eds) *The Polar Twins*. Edinburgh: John Donald. 254–69.

—. 2003–4. "A bit of the other: translation and the Scottish muse in MacDiarmid's poetry" in *Etudes Ecossaises* 9: 105–20.

Stratton, Florence. 1994. *Contemporary African Literature and the Politics of Gender*. London and New York: Routledge.

Todd, Emily B. 1992. "Liz Lochhead interviewed by Emily B. Todd" in *Verse* 8(3)/9(1): 83–95.

Varty, Anne. 1997. "The Mirror and the Vamp: Liz Lochhead" in Gifford, Douglas and Dorothy McMillan (eds) *A History of Scottish Women's Writing*. Edinburgh: Edinburgh University Press. 641–58.

Walker, Alice. 1984. *In Search of Our Mothers' Gardens: Womanist Prose*. New York: Harcourt Brace Jovanovich.

Ward, Margaret. 1983. *Unmanageable Revolutionaries: Women and Irish Nationalism*. London: Pluto Press.

Warner, Marina. 1996. *Monuments and Maidens: The Allegory of the Female Form*. London: Vintage.

Watson, Roderick. 1992. "Visions of Alba: The Constructions of Celtic Roots in Modern Scottish Literature" in *Etudes Ecossaises* 1: 253–64.

Wedderburn, Robert. [c.1550] 1979. *The Complaynt of Scotland* (ed. A.M. Stewart). Edinburgh: Scottish Texts Society.

Whiteford, Eilidh. 1994. "Engendered Subjects: Subjectivity and National Identity in Alasdair Gray's *1982, Janine*" in *Scotlands* 2: 66–82.

Whyte, Christopher. 1995a. "Not(e) from the Margin" in *Chapman* 80: 28–35.

—. (ed.) 1995b. *Gendering the Nation: Studies in Modern Scottish Literature*. Edinburgh: Edinburgh University Press

—. 1995c. "Fishy Masculinities: Neil Gunn's *The Silver Darlings*" in Whyte, Christopher (ed). *Gendering the Nation: Studies in Modern Scottish Literature*. Edinburgh: Edinburgh University Press. 49–68.

Wilson, Rebecca E., and Gillean Somerville-Arjat (eds). 1990. *Sleeping with Monsters: Conversations with Scottish and Irish Women Poets*. Edinburgh: Polygon.

Wittig, Kurt. 1958. *The Scottish Tradition in Literature*. Edinburgh and London: Oliver and Boyd.

Woolf, Virginia. 1938. *Three Guineas*. London: Hogarth Press.

Yeats, William Butler. [1902] 1906. *Cathleen ni Houlihan*. London: Bullen.

—. 1968. *The Variorum Edition of the Poems of W.B. Yeats* (ed. Peter Allt and Russell K. Alspach). New York: MacMillan.

Yuval-Davis, Nira, and Floya Anthias. 1989. *Woman-Nation-State*. Basingstoke: Macmillan.

# Index

Agulhon, Maurice, 25–26
Allan, Dot, 39
Anderson, Benedict, 22, 26, 81–82
Anderson, Carol, 39, 83, 109, 113
Angus, Marion, 39–40
Anthias, Floya, 21, 25, 52, 65, 81
Arnold, Matthew, 39
Atwood, Margaret, 73–74
Banks, Iain, 114
Barbour, John, 28
Barker, Elspeth, 23
Baxter, William, 92
Berec, Laurent, 65
Blok, Alexander, 42–43
Boadicea. *See* Boudicca
Boethius, Anicius Manlius Severinus, 31
Boland, Eavan, 110, 113
Boleyn, Anne, 102
Boudicca, 17
Boyd, S.J., 102, 106
Boyd, William, 111
Browne, Thomas, 103
Bruce, George, 39
Burns, Robert, 12, 27–34 *passim*, 77, 96
Buthlay, Kenneth, 42
Butler, Judith, 83
Byron, George Gordon, Lord, 98
Camden, William, 17
Carlyle, Thomas, 27, 47
Carswell, Catherine, 40
Carter, Angela, 97
Chapman, Malcolm, 85
Chartier, Alain, 31
Corkery, Daniel, 45–46
Cowan, Edward J., 32
Craig, Cairns, 104, 122–123, 125
Crawford, Thomas, 51, 58
Cruickshank, Helen, 39–40, 54
Daniels, Stephen, 20
Diamond, Sara, 73
Dickson, Beth, 60
Donne, John, 91
Drayton, Michael, 17, 20, 30–31, 65
Dudley, Robert, Lord Leicester, 102

Dunn, Douglas, 27–30, 123
Eliot, T.S., 103
Elizabeth I (Queen of England), 16, 21, 100–102
Ewing, Winnie, 54
Frame, Ronald, 111
Galford, Ellen, 14, 112–13, 115–16
Galloway, Janice, 14, 111–14 passim, 122–26
Garioch, Robert, 35
Gellner, Ernest, 20, 81
Gheeraerts, Marcus (the Younger), 16
Gibbon, Lewis Grassic, 13, 22, 27, 35–39, 48–55, 58, 62, 87, 106, 109, 117, 123
Gibson, Mel, 76
Gifford, Douglas, 9, 32, 70
Gilbert, Sandra, 97, 99
Gittings, Christopher, 70
Godwin, William, 92
Graves, Robert, 34
Gray, Alasdair, 13–14, 15, 23–24, 28, 53, 68–77, 87–99, 102, 104–7, 124, 126
Grieve, Christopher Murray. *See* MacDiarmid, Hugh
Gubar, Susan, 97, 99
Gunn, Neil, 35–36, 38–39, 48, 51–53, 55, 109
Hagemann, Susanne, 84–85, 112–14
Harvie, Christopher, 19, 49
Hay, George Campbell, 45
Hendry, Joy, 78, 83
Henry VIII (King of England), 102
Hobbes, Thomas, 90–91
Hogg, James, 27–28, 95
hooks, bell, 79
Jacob, Violet, 39–40
James VI and I (King of Scotland and England), 17
Jayawardena, Kumari, 81
Kennedy, A.L., 14, 116–22, 126
Kerrigan, Catherine, 28–29, 53
Knox, John, 100
Kolodny, Annette, 24
Kreis, Georg, 29

Lant, Antonia, 25
Lasker-Schüler, Else, 42
Linklater, Eric, 39
Lochhead, Liz, 14, 79, 96–102, 106, 114
Lodge, David, 71
Longley, Edna, 123
MacCaig, Norman, 35
MacDiarmid, Hugh, 13–16, 23, 27, 33, 35–49, 54, 59, 68, 87, 100, 103–4, 107, 109, 113–14, 126
MacDiarmid, Valda, 54
MacIntyre, Duncan Bàn, 59
Mackay Brown, George, 35
MacLean, Sorley, 45, 47
March, Cristie Leigh, 124
Markievicz, Constance Georgine (Countess Markievicz), 37
Mary I (Queen of England), 100
Mary, Queen of Scots, 27, 100–102
Massie, Alan, 111
McCarey, Peter, 44
McMillan, Dorothy, 111
Mitchell, James Leslie. *See* Gibbon, Lewis Grassic
Mitchison, Naomi, 13–14, 39–40, 54–55, 58–63, 67, 113–14, 126
Moffat, Alexander, 35
Morgan, Edwin, 35
Morton, Brian, 51
Muir, Edwin, 39–40, 104
Muir, Willa, 14, 40, 54–58, 62–63, 67, 126
Muldoon, Paul, 123
Nairn, Tom, 38, 104
Norquay, Glenda, 39, 83, 109, 113, 123
O'Hegarty, P.S., 37
O'Rathaille, Aodhagan, 45, 48
Paisley, Janet, 75–77
Plato, 90
Poe, Edgar Allan, 95
Price, Richard, 53
Pushkin, Alexander, 105
Ramsay, Allan (poet), 33
Reizbaum, Marilyn, 39, 78, 80
Renan, Ernest, 39
Rich, Adrienne, 97

Richardson, Thomas, 49
Rilke, Rainer Maria, 48
Rose, Gillian, 23
Ross, Alexander, 33–34
Sampson, Anthony, 91
Schama, Simon, 23
Schumann, Clara, 122
Schumann, Robert, 122
Scott, Walter, Sir, 22–23, 28, 39, 58, 105
Sedgwick, Eve Kosofsky, 82
Shaw, George Bernard, 95
Shelley, Harriet, 92
Shelley, Mary, 88, 92– 99 *passim*
Shelley, Percy Bysshe, 92, 98
Showalter, Elaine, 84, 85
Smith, G. Gregory, 13, 14, 102–3, 107
Smith, Sydney Goodsir, 39
Soutar, William, 39
Straet, Jan van der, 65
Stratton, Florence, 67
Thatcher, Margaret, 12, 115
Trevlyn, Valda. *See* MacDiarmid, Valda
Tudor, Mary. *See* Mary I (Queen of England)
Urquhart, Thomas, 103
Vespucci, Amerigo, 65
Victoria I (Queen of the United Kingdom), 17
Warner, Alan, 112
Warner, Marina, 12, 18–19, 26, 48, 51, 58, 65, 100, 124
Watson, Roderick, 53
Wedderburn, Robert, 30–32, 67
Wells, H.G., 95
Welsh, Irvine, 112, 114
Whiteford, Eilidh, 69
Whyte, Christopher, 9, 23, 49, 52, 54, 70, 83–84
Wittig, Kurt, 38–39, 49
Wollstonecraft, Mary, 92
Woolf, Virginia, 79, 99
Yeats, William Butler, 36–37, 45, 51
Young, Douglas, 39
Yuval-Davis, Nira, 21, 25, 52, 65, 81